D0844189

Rulers of Ancient Egypt

Other Books in the History Makers Series:

History MAKERS

Rulers of Ancient Egypt

By Russell Roberts

Lucent Books
P.O. Box 289011, San Diego, CA 92198-9011

Library of Congress Cataloging-in-Publication Data

Roberts, Russell, 1953–
    Rulers of ancient Egypt / by Russell Roberts.
        p.   cm. — (History makers)
    Includes bibliographical references (p.   ) and index.
    Summary: Discusses five famous and influential leaders of ancient
Egypt. Included are Queen Hatshepsut, Akhenaten, Tutankhamon,
Ramses II, and Cleopatra.
    ISBN 1-56006-438-2 (lib : alk. paper)
    1. Pharaohs—Biography—Juvenile literature.   2. Egypt—Kings and
rulers—Biography—Juvenile literature. 3. Egypt—History—To 640
A.D.—Juvenile literature. 4. Egypt—Antiquities—Juvenile
literature.   [1. Kings, queens, rulers, etc. 2. Egypt—
Antiquities. 3. Egypt—History—To 640 A.D.]   I. Title.
II. Series.
DT83.R56   1999
932'.009'9
[b]—dc21   98-35271
                                                                CIP
                                                                 AC

CONTENTS

FOREWORD

The literary form most often referred to as "multiple biography" was perfected in the first century A.D. by Plutarch, a perceptive and talented moralist and historian who hailed from the small town of Chaeronea in central Greece. His most famous work, *Parallel Lives*, consists of a long series of biographies of noteworthy ancient Greek and Roman statesmen and military leaders. Frequently, Plutarch compares a famous Greek to a famous Roman, pointing out similarities in personality and achievements. These expertly constructed and very readable tracts provided later historians and others, including playwrights like Shakespeare, with priceless information about prominent ancient personages and also inspired new generations of writers to tackle the multiple biography genre.

The Lucent History Makers series proudly carries on the venerable tradition handed down from Plutarch. Each volume in the series consists of a set of six to eight biographies of important and influential historical figures who were linked together by a common factor. In *Rulers of Ancient Rome*, for example, all the figures were generals, consuls, or emperors of either the Roman Republic or Empire; while the subjects of *Fighters Against American Slavery*, though they lived in different places and times, all shared the same goal, namely the eradication of human servitude. Mindful that politicians and military leaders are not (and never have been) the only people who shape the course of history, the editors of the series have also included representatives from a wide range of endeavors, including scientists, artists, writers, philosophers, religious leaders, and sports figures.

Each book is intended to give a range of figures—some well known, others less known; some who made a great impact on history, others who made only a small impact. For instance, by making Columbus's initial voyage possible, Spain's Queen Isabella I, featured in *Women Leaders of Nations*, helped to open up the New World to exploration and exploitation by the European powers. Unarguably, therefore, she made a major contribution to a series of events that had momentous consequences for the entire world. By contrast, Catherine II, the eighteenth-century Russian queen, and Golda Meir, the modern Israeli prime minister, did not play roles of global impact; however, their policies and actions significantly influenced the historical development of both their own countries and their regional neighbors. Regardless of their relative importance in the greater historical scheme, all of the figures chronicled in the History Makers series made contributions to posterity; and their public achievements, as well as what is known about their private lives, are presented and evaluated in light of the most recent scholarship.

In addition, each volume in the series is documented and substantiated by a wide array of primary and secondary source quotations. The primary source quotes enliven the text by presenting eyewitness views of the times and culture in which each history maker lived; while the secondary source quotes, taken from the works of respected modern scholars, offer expert elaboration and/or critical commentary. Each quote is footnoted, demonstrating to the reader exactly where biographers find their information. The footnotes also provide the reader with the means of conducting additional research. Finally, to further guide and illuminate readers, each volume in the series features photographs, two bibliographies, and a comprehensive index.

The History Makers series provides both students engaged in research and more casual readers with informative, enlightening, and entertaining overviews of individuals from a variety of circumstances, professions, and backgrounds. No doubt all of them, whether loved or hated, benevolent or cruel, constructive or destructive, will remain endlessly fascinating to each new generation seeking to identify the forces that shaped their world.

An Extraordinary Civilization

The history of ancient Egypt spans over three thousand years. During much of that time the country was ruled autocratically by kings, or pharaohs. In an attempt to impose some order on the vast number of kings who ruled Egypt, historians separated them into dynasties, which are groups of leaders related by marriage or birth. Thirty dynasties existed during Egypt's long and often turbulent history.

As might be expected during such a long period (by comparison, as an independent nation the United States is less than 250 years old), Egypt experienced every possible type of ruler: good, bad, mediocre, average, indifferent, focused, weak, strong, kind, and cruel.

For over three thousand years, a succession of kings, or pharaohs, wielded absolute power in ancient Egypt.

Of course, just as modern countries change throughout their history according to the influence of both internal and external forces, so too did ancient Egypt. At first Egypt's rulers had little desire to expand beyond their own borders. Gradually, however, this attitude changed; more peoples from other lands and other kingdoms began coming into contact with Egypt, either through peaceful or nonpeaceful means, and the country's leaders realized that they could not remain isolated in the Nile valley forever. The pharaohs steadily expanded their power and influence on the world around them until, finally, they were the masters of a large empire stretching far beyond the Nile valley. Eventually even this glorious era passed, and the country steadily declined in power and prestige until it finally lost its independence altogether under the Romans.

While it lasted, however, Egypt's era of empire produced some of the best and most well known rulers in its history. Ramses II, called Ramses the Great, fought a critical battle against the Hit-

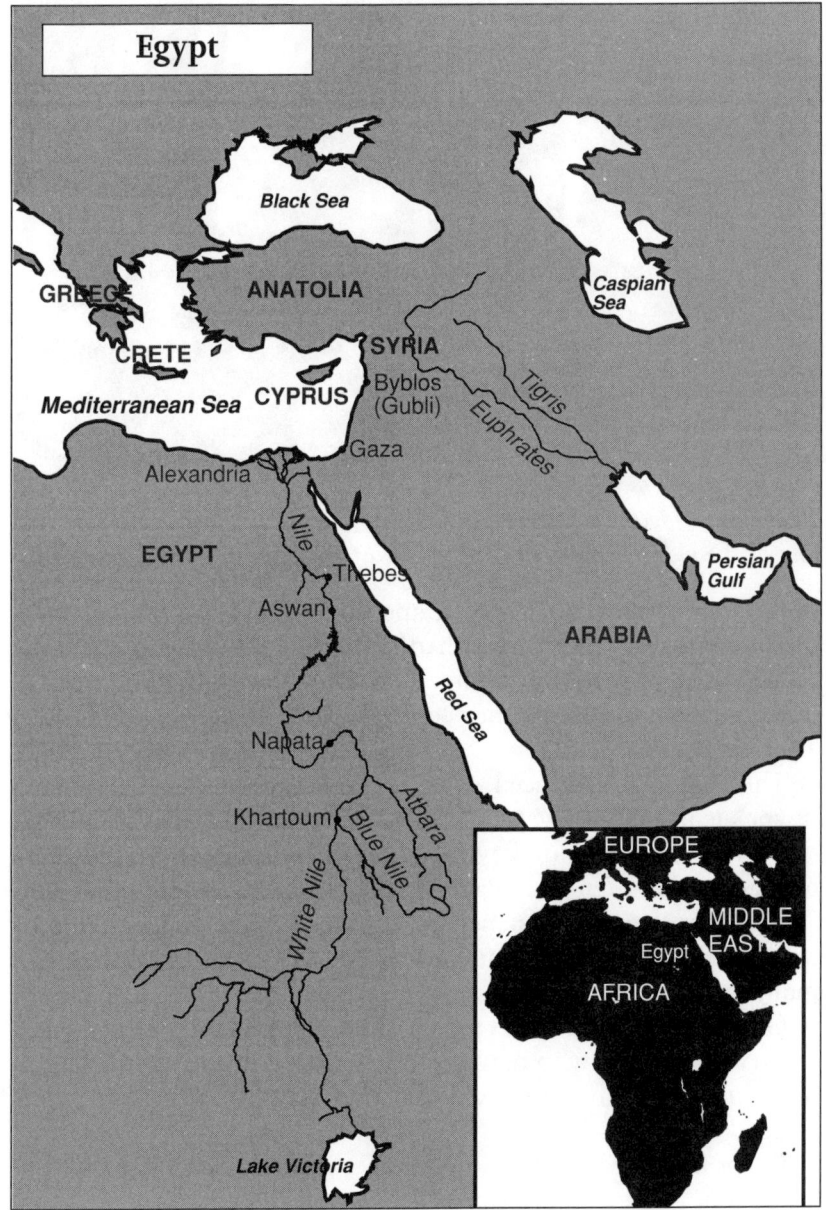

The temple at Abu Simbel, built during the reign of Ramses the Great, is one of the many architectural wonders of the ancient Egyptian world.

tites, lived to be almost ninety, and covered the country with his monuments. Another pharaoh of this period was the boy-king, Tutankhamon, who did not live long enough to make much of an impact during his life but has certainly made his presence felt long after his death.

This era also produced some of the most intriguing kings in Egypt's lengthy history. One was Akhenaten, who tried to change two thousand years of Egyptian religious tradition by installing one god—the Aten—in place of the many that had been worshiped. Another was Hatshepsut, the queen who became king by possibly stealing the throne and then had herself portrayed as a man, complete with the pharaoh's false beard.

Of course, other periods also had notable rulers. One is the legendary Cleopatra, who may or may not have been beautiful but is noteworthy because she was the last ruler of an independent Egypt.

Egypt had many notable rulers over its long history. These five are among the most interesting.

CHAPTER 1

Ancient Egypt

Long before the birth of Christ and the legendary civilizations of Greece and Rome, there was Egypt.

For thousands of years Egypt was the most advanced country in the ancient world. Egyptian achievements in art, medicine, architecture, communications, agriculture, and other fields were not equaled anywhere else in the world for centuries. Long after their society had vanished, visitors from other countries in the ancient world came to Egypt and marveled at its accomplishments. When the Greek historian Herodotus visited Egypt in the fifth century B.C., he wrote in awe about how the country "contains works which are more remarkable than those of any other land."[1]

Today, the words of Herodotus still apply. Despite everything that modern society has achieved, humanity still stands with heads bowed at the altar of Egyptian accomplishment. Even though much of Egypt's past remains buried, it is clear that the civilization that flourished along the banks of the Nile was one of the most remarkable the world has ever produced.

Egypt was the most advanced culture in the ancient world. It achieved unequaled advances in architecture and science and amassed a large empire centuries before the rise of Greece and Rome.

The Nile's Gift

Without the Nile River, Egypt would not exist. This is why Herodotus called Egypt "the gift of the Nile."[2]

Unlike other countries, Egypt has neither large mountains, great plains, nor vast green fields. What it does have is a narrow strip of fertile land approximately seven hundred miles long and just a few miles wide, extending on both sides of the Nile. This is the river's gift of life to Egypt.

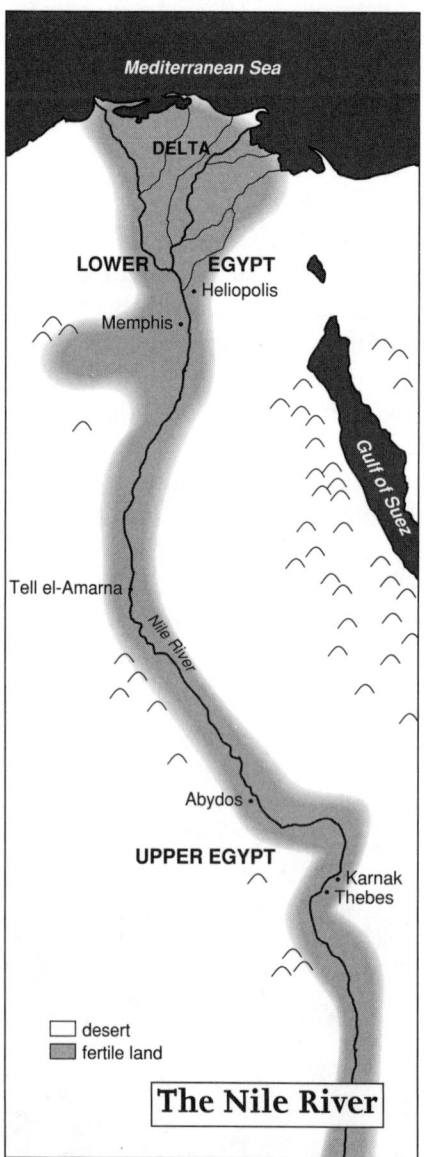

The Nile River

Each year when the star Sirius was seen at dawn above the horizon (in late June or early July), the Nile rose, flooding the land around it during what was called the inundation. After it receded in late September or early October, the river left behind a fertile black silt. Since no other part of Egypt's desert soil was suitable for agriculture, farming communities sprang up along the Nile. When the Nile did not rise far enough, Egyptian harvests (wheat, barley, fruits, and vegetables) were poor; when it swelled too much, the high water destroyed dikes and other agricultural aids, forcing farmers to rebuild.

Because of the dramatic difference in soil types, Egyptians divided their country into two regions: They called the part that could be cultivated the black land, and the desert the red land. The foreboding desert climate allowed Egypt to remain isolated for centuries, knowing little of the world outside, and protected by the vast expanses of rock and sand surrounding the Nile valley.

Politically, Egypt was also a country divided. From Aswan to the Mediterranean Sea, the Nile flows from south to north. Thus, Upper Egypt is actually the southern portion of the country and Lower Egypt is the northern part, near where the Nile splits into channels to reach the Mediterranean (this area is called the Nile Delta). According to Egyptian tradition, these two sections were united into one country by King Menes (or Narmer) of Upper Egypt around 3000 B.C. However, the memory of the divisions remained in the designation of the pharaoh as "the King of Upper and Lower Egypt."

Many of the Egyptian gods had the qualities of both humans and animals. The god Sobek, patron of the pharaohs, had the body of a man and the head of a crocodile.

Religion

Religion was an important part of an Egyptian's everyday life. (Herodotus said they were "religious to excess, beyond any other nation in the world."[3]) Although Egypt had many gods, ordinary people were considered unpure and were not allowed inside the great temples. Instead, people worshiped small statues of the gods that they kept in their homes. The only interaction common citizens had with the temple gods was during religious festivals, when a holy statue was taken outside to be seen by all.

The government controlled the major temples, and the pharaoh supported them through donations of goods, valuables, slaves, and food. The temples became wealthy, and the temple priests grew into a powerful political force as vast bureaucracies evolved to run the shrines. During the twelfth century B.C., for example, over one hundred thousand people worked for the temple of Amon at Karnak.

Early in Egypt's history, the gods were based on natural phenomena and creatures, such as the wind, sun, lions, and crocodiles. Gradually the gods took on human qualities, and their forms began to resemble people. However, sometimes they still retained their animal heads. For instance, the god Sobek was portrayed as a man with a crocodile's head.

The pharaoh (the word means "great house") was thought to be descended from the gods. He was considered a bridge between the world of mortals and the world of gods; through his earthly existence, he could bring harmony to the relationship between gods, humanity, and natural forces.

Death and Mummification

Death was a very important part of religion to the Egyptians. This was not because they were a gloomy people but rather because they were confident that the afterlife was going to be even better than their time on earth.

The Egyptians believed that numerous spirits were released when a person died. The most meaningful were the *ba*, which is similar to today's conception of a soul, and the *ka*, which was the life force. It was necessary for a body to survive after death in a form that both the *ba* and *ka* could recognize so that they could reunite with it in the afterlife. This is what gave rise to mummification.

When Herodotus visited Egypt, he watched the mummification process and wrote the only eyewitness account on record:

> In the best treatment, first of all they draw out the brains through the nostrils with an iron hook. . . . Next they make an incision in the flank with a sharp obsidian blade through which they can extract all the internal organs. Then they clean out the body cavity, rinsing it with palm wine. . . . [Then] they cover the corpse with natron [a natural salt that dried out the body but still left it flexible] for seventy days, but for no longer, and so mummify it. After the seventy days are up they wash the corpse and wrap it from head to toe in bandages of the finest linen anointed with gum.[4]

All of the internal organs except the heart were embalmed separately and placed in small containers called canopic jars. The heart was returned to the body, since the mummy needed it in the afterlife. Hundreds of yards of linen were used to wrap the body. A lifelike mummy mask was often employed so that if the head was lost or damaged, the *ba* could recognize the mummy by its mask.

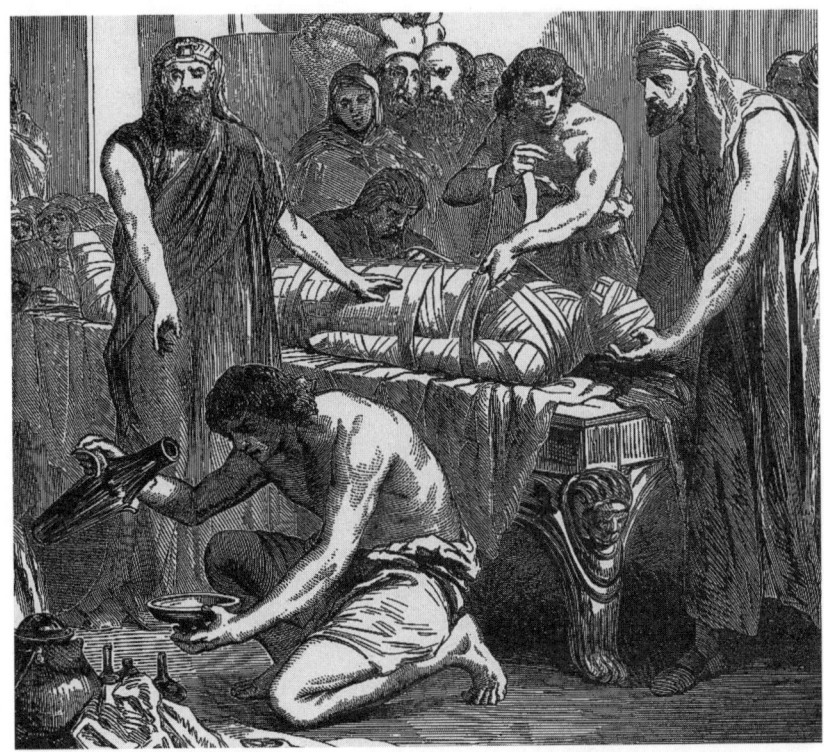

The Egyptians mummified the corpses of their dead because they believed that the ba, *or soul, would be reunited with the body in the afterlife.*

In the afterlife the mummy faced the moment of ultimate judgment in the Hall of Two Truths, when its heart was weighed against the ostrich feather of Ma'at, the goddess of truth, order, and law. If the mummy had led a bad life, its heart would be heavier than the feather, and it would be thrown to Ammit, a monster with a crocodile's head, who ate it. This destroyed the soul. But if the heart and feather weighed the same, it was the sign of a just life, and the mummy would live forever.

The Kingdoms

Egyptian history is divided into several periods. The oldest is the Early Dynastic Period, approximately 3150 to 2686 B.C. This was followed by the Old Kingdom (2686–2181 B.C.), the Middle Kingdom (2040–1782 B.C.), and the New Kingdom (1570–1070 B.C.). Both the Old and Middle Kingdoms were followed by periods when Egypt was in turmoil, plagued by civil war, invasion, and even foreign rule. These periods are called the First Intermediate

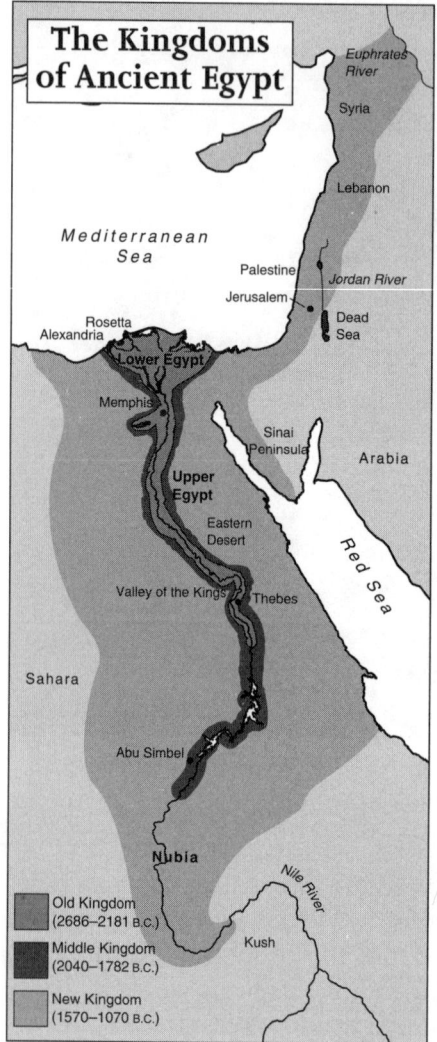

The Kingdoms of Ancient Egypt

Old Kingdom
(2686–2181 B.C.)

Middle Kingdom
(2040–1782 B.C.)

New Kingdom
(1570–1070 B.C.)

Period (2181–2040 B.C.) and the Second Intermediate Period (1782–1570 B.C.). After the New Kingdom ended, the country began a long, slow decline in power and prestige that culminated in annexation by Rome in 27 B.C.

The Old Kingdom began with the Third Dynasty. Egyptian rulers are divided into dynasties, which are groups of leaders related by either marriage or birth. Altogether there are thirty dynasties, and rulers are often identified by their dynasty. For example, Ramses II is identified by the Nineteenth Dynasty.

The Old Kingdom

The Old Kingdom was a glorious period for Egypt. The country made great advances in medicine, mathematics, astronomy, and engineering.

The practice of medicine in Egypt was a curious combination of science and magic. Thanks to mummification, some aspects of Egyptian medicine were highly advanced. Doctors understood how the body worked, and some of their treatments for common ailments, including stitching deep cuts and splinting fractured bones, are the same as modern medicine. Remarkably, doctors also possessed sophisticated health knowledge, such as the necessity of hygiene and cleanliness in treating illness and disease. Yet magic spells and rituals were also part of Egyptian medicine; these were often invoked when doctors were faced with illnesses in which the symptoms were difficult to diagnose.

In the field of mathematics, the Egyptians developed a simple type of arithmetic that they used to measure their fields. This enabled them to estimate yields of grain so that they would know if harvests would be sufficient. Mathematics was also important in the computations used to build the pyramids, temples, and other structures. By combining mathematics with a knowledge of astronomy and the movements of the sun, the Egyptians devised a solar calendar of twelve thirty-day months plus five days that was more accurate than anything that would be used in the world for the next several centuries.

The development of writing signaled the birth of a new era of communications for the world. Egyptians developed a series of picture signs called hieroglyphs (from a Greek term meaning "sacred carvings") into a form of handwriting, and paper was devised from the papyrus reed. The advent of writing meant that the tools of a centralized government, including records, instructions, and the like, were no longer dependent on memory and could be recorded and passed along to future generations. The very elements that make up a civilization—stories, poems, songs—could also now be put down in black and white.

Unfortunately, the Old Kingdom ended in chaos. Pharaoh Pepi II of the Sixth Dynasty reigned for ninety years, and as his authority weakened in his final years, the country was filled with unrest. Historically, strong rulers were necessary for Egypt to thrive; when they were absent, and the power of the central government

Egypt was the first civilization to develop writing. The picture signs, or hieroglyphs, seen here tell the story of the sun's daily journey through Egypt.

faltered, the country broke down. Soon after Pepi II's death in 2184 B.C., Egypt was torn by civil war. Princes and kings of various Egyptian provinces fought for control as the country split into various factions.

"This land is helter-skelter," bemoaned a writer at the time. "I show thee a land topsy-turvy. . . . I show thee the son as foe, the brother as an enemy, and a man killing his father."[5]

The Middle Kindgom

After these years of chaos—known as the First Intermediate Period, which lasted for almost two centuries—Egypt was reunited by Pharaoh Mentuhotep in 2040 B.C. Mentuhotep's reign began both the Eleventh Dynasty and the Middle Kingdom. Eschewing the former capital of Memphis, Mentuhotep chose his own city of Thebes as the country's new capital.

During the Middle Kingdom, Egyptian influence spread into Nubia and Palestine, and the country was again prosperous. But by the middle of the Thirteenth Dynasty, Egypt was saddled with a series of weak and ineffectual kings. This set the stage for the Second Intermediate Period, during which the country again splintered among various factions due to the lack of a strong central government.

Taking advantage of the confusion within the country, a people called the Hyksos, who had come from Palestine and settled in the Nile Delta, used the horse-drawn chariot—a weapon the isolated Egyptians had never seen and were powerless against—to take control of much of Egypt in 1640 B.C. On their speedy chariots, the Hyksos were able to ride among the ranks of Egyptian foot soldiers, inflict heavy losses, and quickly retreat, leaving disaster and confusion in their wake.

Beginning with the Seventeenth Dynasty, a group of kings from Thebes, having mastered the use of the horse-drawn chariot themselves, led a revolt against the Hyksos that ultimately drove them from the country.

The New Kingdom

The Eighteenth Dynasty began the four-hundred-year period known as the New Kingdom, Egypt's most celebrated era. Included in the Eighteenth and Nineteenth Dynasties are some of the most famous names in Egyptian history, such as Thutmose III, Hatshepsut, Akhenaten, Tutankhamon, Seti, and Ramses the Great. The New Kingdom was a time of empire and prosperity; Egypt was the undisputed master of the ancient world. As tribute poured into Egypt from its conquered lands, the pharaohs embarked on massive and expensive building projects.

A Slow Decline

Eventually this period also ended, and the country began a slow decline as a world power. The last great pharaoh in Egyptian history was Ramses III, second king of the Twentieth Dynasty in the New Kingdom. During his reign, which lasted from approximately 1182 to 1151 B.C., he reestablished the authority of the monarchy, which had been waning in the face of the priesthood's growing power and influence. He also fought a series of military campaigns to keep the country safe from foreign invaders, particularly the "Sea Peoples," the peoples of various ethnic backgrounds who came from across the Mediterranean Sea and threatened to overwhelm Egypt. Although Ramses successfully defended Egypt's borders, its empire was lost. An inscription describes the difficulties he faced:

> The foreign countries made a conspiracy in their islands. . . .
> No land could stand before their arms, beginning with Khatti
> [the Hittites] and Alasiya [Cyprus]. . . . A camp was set up in

After mastering the use of the horse-drawn chariot, a group of Egyptian kings from the Seventeenth Dynasty drove the invading Hyksos—who came from Palestine—from Egypt.

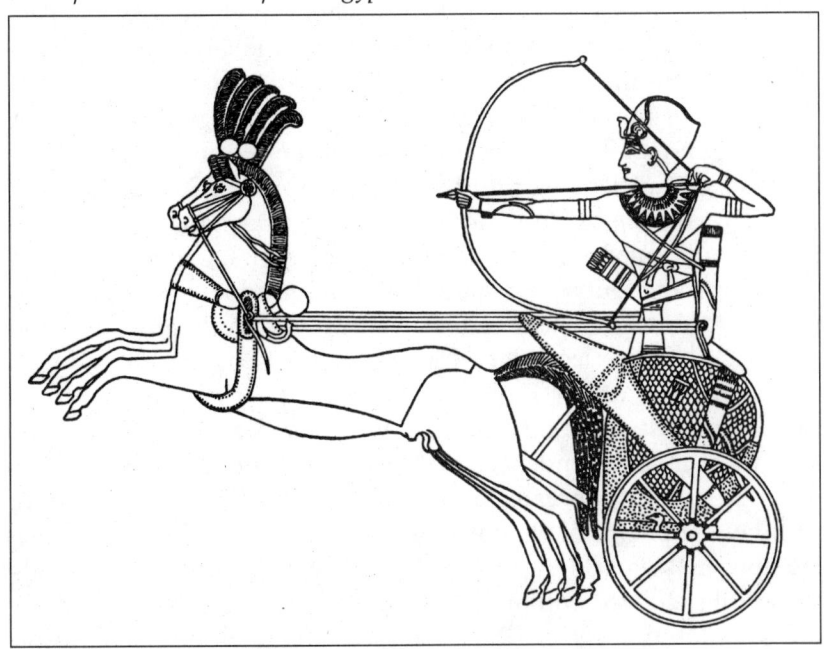

one place in Amor [Syria]. They desolated its people, and its land was like that which has never come into being. They were coming forward toward Egypt, while the flame was prepared before them.[6]

Thanks to Ramses III, Egypt saved itself; however, the effort sapped the country's strength. With the empire in tatters and the source of its great wealth gone, Egypt was seized by economic chaos. Problems became so severe that the workers on the royal tombs staged the first recorded strike in history when their monthly food rations were overdue.

A dreary parade of ineffectual kings struggled with the priests at Thebes for control of the country. The Amon temple at Karnak alone owned and managed more than 240,000 hectares (almost 600,000 acres) of fertile farmland. Eventually Egypt split in two once again; Upper Egypt was ruled from Thebes and Lower Egypt from the city of Tanis in the Nile Delta.

Finally in about 720 B.C., the Sudanese marched up from the south and conquered most of Egypt. They were followed in the first half of the seventh century B.C. by the Assyrians, who devastated Thebes, the legendary city of Egyptian power.

"Thebes in its entirety I conquered," said the Assyrian king Ashurbanipal. "Silver, gold, precious stones, all the possessions of the palace . . . I took away from Thebes."[7]

The Assyrians were vanquished by Persia in about 525 B.C. Persia ruled Egypt until 332, when Alexander the Great from Macedonia overran the Persian Empire.

Alexander founded the city of Alexandria in Egypt but did not live long enough to see it become one of the leading metropolitan areas of the ancient world. After his death in 323, the Egyptian throne was taken by Ptolemy Soter, one of his generals. He and his descendants ruled Egypt for the next 250 years. The official language of the country became Greek, and gradually the language and traditions of ancient Egypt were forgotten by all except the priests. When the legendary Cleopatra came to the throne in 51 B.C. as the last of the Ptolemaic dynasty, the glory of pharaonic Egypt was just a distant memory. With her death in the year 30, Egypt lost its independence and became a Roman province.

As Christianity spread throughout the world, the last surviving members of pharaonic Egypt took refuge on the tiny island of Philae above Aswan. Here, in the Temple of Isis, the ancient rituals were still practiced and hieroglyphics still read. But when the temple was closed in A.D. 550, it was the death knell of a civilization that had existed for over three thousand years. The images of the gods were vandalized, the priests were forced to flee, and countless papyrus rolls were burned, wiping out all traces of Egyptian culture and knowledge.

The glory of pharaonic Egypt came to an end with the arrival of Alexander the Great in 332 B.C. Over the next 250 years Egypt would be more influenced by Greek culture than its own.

For the next thirteen hundred years, pharaonic Egypt was lost to history. Visitors to the country marveled at the mighty pyramids and other wondrous structures, but the hieroglyphics were a mystery to them, and so the secrets of Egypt remained hidden.

Egypt Rediscovered

Under Napoléon Bonaparte, French soldiers accidentally discovered the Rosetta Stone in 1799. Eventually, the stone allowed scholars to decipher the ancient hieroglyphics and uncover the long-buried secrets of Egypt's past.

When Napoléon Bonaparte of France invaded Egypt in 1798, he brought with him two hundred scholars and researchers to study the civilization of ancient Egypt. Although the French military forces were defeated after just three years, the scholars returned to France and published their findings. These works described many of the wonders that the French scientists had seen and visited, but without a way to read the strange writing on the walls and the temples, the story behind ancient Egypt was still unknown.

The key to unlocking the mysteries of Egypt was held by a broken slab of black basalt, which was discovered by French soldiers digging trenches near Rashid, or Rosetta, in 1799. On the stone was an inscription praising Ptolemy V, written in 196 B.C. What was important, however, was that the same inscription was written three ways: in hieroglyphics, demotic characters, and Greek. Researchers knew that if they could translate all three inscriptions, they might crack the secrets of Egyptian hieroglyphics.

For over two decades scientists struggled to decipher the inscription using the Rosetta stone. Finally, in 1822, a French scholar of ancient languages, Jean-François Champollion, broke the code by translating a single word—"Ptolmys"—in the hieroglyphics. After more than a thousand years, the language of ancient Egypt was finally able to be read and understood again.

As the knowledge of what lay buried beneath the desert sands spread, many people came to Egypt during the nineteenth century. Some were scholars, but many were treasure hunters hoping for fabulous finds of gold and precious gems. In their quest for

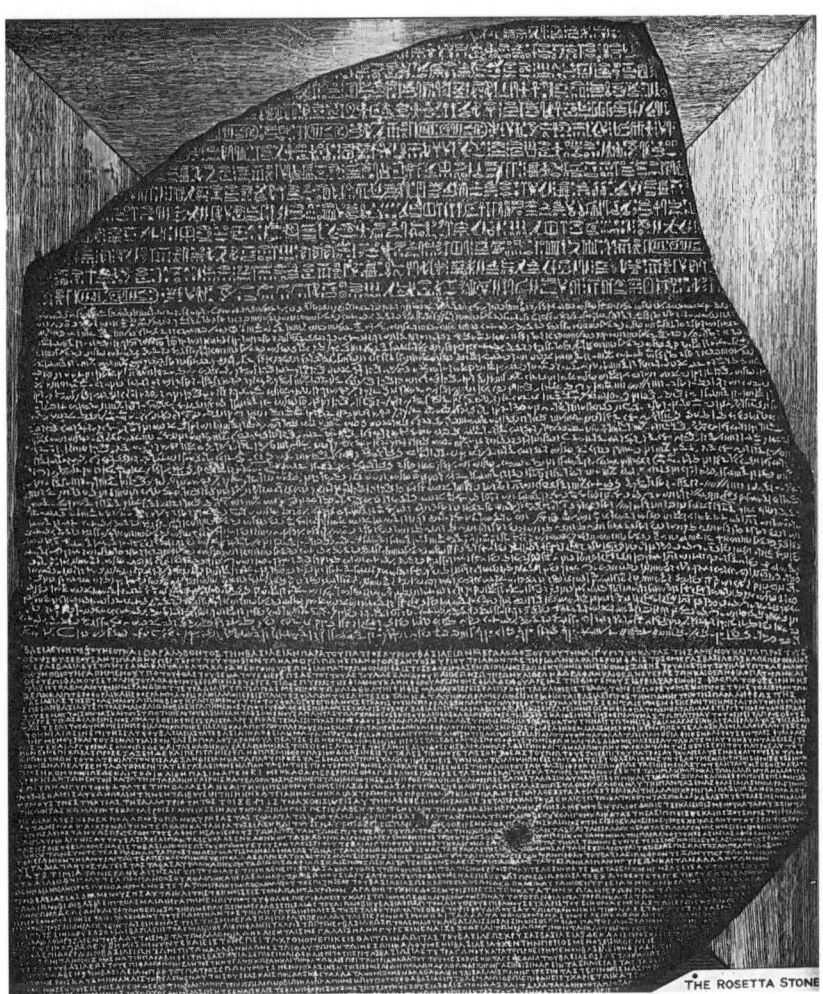

THE ROSETTA STONE

The Rosetta Stone contained a passage written in three languages: Greek, demotic characters, and hieroglyphics. It took scholars more than twenty years to unlock the mysteries of the hieroglyphics.

money, tombs were opened hastily and clumsily, often with battering rams and gunpowder; many valuable antiquities were destroyed in the frantic search for wealth. One explorer, Giovanni Battista Belzoni, published a book about his adventures in tombs and pyramids, including how he would accidentally crush mummies as he walked through tombs.

Gradually, however, serious scientists replaced the treasure hunters, and the search for tombs and relics was done professionally and properly through archaeological digs using delicate tools and instruments. Humanity was at last able to begin discovering the fascinating civilization of ancient Egypt.

CHAPTER 2

"His Majesty, Herself": Queen Hatshepsut

She was, according to Egyptologist James Henry Breasted, "the first great woman in history."[8]

This is just one of many accolades for Queen Hatshepsut, an intelligent, ambitious woman in the predominantly male world of ancient Egypt who ultimately became ruler of the most powerful nation on the earth. By the way she maneuvered through the male-dominated power structure, as well as the manner in which she ruled Egypt for more than twenty years, Hatshepsut set an example for every other female monarch throughout history.

To anyone who knew her father, the likelihood that Hatshepsut would take the crown of Egypt for herself would not have come as a surprise. Few pharaohs were as bold and daring as Thutmose I.

Thutmose I was the third sovereign of the Eighteenth Dynasty, the same dynasty that finally drove the Hyksos out of Egypt, reunited the country, and ushered in an unprecedented era of empire, wealth, and power called the New Kingdom.

A born fighter—on one campaign he was so anxious to get into battle that he was "raging like a panther"[9]—Thutmose led the Egyptian armies farther north than ever before. He conquered a vast empire that included Nubia, Syria, and Palestine, and he compiled a string of military victories. As a scribe wrote, "His Majesty sailed downstream with all countries in his grasp."[10] Ultimately, no monarch or nation dared oppose the armed might of Egypt.

Thutmose had four children by his royal wife, Ahmose, but only Hatshepsut—whose name means "chieftainess of noble women"—survived childhood. Her sister, Akhbetneferu, died in infancy, and her two brothers, Wadjmose and Amenmose, both died in their late teens. Obviously both sons preceded their father in death, or else one of them would have succeeded to his throne. There is also the possibility that Thutmose had a third son, named Ramose, but he, too, apparently died before his father.

Hatshepsut's father, Thutmose I, was a fierce warrior who extended Egypt's territorial holdings into Syria, Nubia, and Palestine. He died without a male heir to the throne.

As an infant, Hatshepsut was cared for by a nurse named Sitre, also known as Inet. A badly damaged sandstone statue shows Hatshepsut sitting on her nurse's knee. Since Hatshepsut commissioned a statue of this nurse, she must have been fond of her.

According to biographer Evelyn Wells, as Hatshepsut matured she wore male clothing, in part to ease her father's grief at the loss of his royal sons. (He had other sons by the minor wives and concubines normally available to a pharaoh.)

Marriage and Power

Thutmose I died when Hatshepsut was twelve. It was then that she married her half brother, Thutmose II, who had been selected to succeed her father as pharaoh. Brother and sister marriages were common practice among Egyptian royalty, for it kept the throne "in the family" and enabled the royal line to continue. It also enabled Hatshepsut to remain close to the seat of power after her father died.

Thutmose II was as different from Hatshepsut's dynamic warrior father as night is different from day. An examination of Thutmose II's mummy reveals an overweight man with narrow shoulders, whose body lacked both vigor and muscular power. Whereas many kings were bald, Thutmose II had long hair that appeared to have been curled by artificial means (such as some type of early curling iron). This has led to speculation that he was effeminate. While this is unknown, when compared with the vigorous fighters Thutmose I and Thutmose III, Thutmose II seems lacking.

When her husband, Thutmose II, died, Hatshepsut was named regent of Egypt until the infant Thutmose III—Thutmose II's son by a concubine—reached the proper age to assume the throne.

Historians speculate that the marriage of Hatshepsut and the apparently weak and non-aggressive Thutmose II was forged by the iron-willed Hatshepsut herself so that she could be the power behind the throne while pretending to defer to her husband. While Thutmose II fulfilled the male-oriented role of pharaoh, Hatshepsut could run Egypt, which she might have felt was her right and destiny as the full-blooded heir of the mighty Thutmose I.

Indeed, this image of the ambitious Hatshepsut is prevalent throughout Egyptology. As historian Peter A. Clayton writes, "As Tuthmosis [Thutmose] II had realized early on, Hatshepsut was a strong-willed woman who would not let anyone or anything stand in her way."[11]

Other Egyptologists, however, disagree with this portrayal. Joyce Tyldesley writes, "Nor is there any proof to support the assumption that during the reign of the supposedly sickly Tuthmosis II it was Hatchepsut, the power behind the throne, who ruled Egypt."[12]

Hatshepsut Becomes Pharaoh

For a long time it was thought that Hatshepsut bore Thutmose two daughters but no sons. However, Tyldesley says that the marriage produced just one child, the princess Neferure. After her father's death, Neferure began to appear in public more, and it is possible that Hatshepsut was grooming her to play an important role in the life of the royal family. Her primary role, however, was that of marrying the next pharaoh, but this was a part that Neferure would never play. She died before a marriage could take place.

Thutmose II ruled for approximately ten years. When he died (apparently from a skin disease) in about 1504 B.C., his son by a concubine, Isit, became Pharaoh Thutmose III. However, Thutmose III was just a young child, and possibly even an infant, upon his succession to the throne. Hatshepsut, at this time in her early to mid-twenties, became regent for the young king.

To an ambitious, intelligent woman like Hatshepsut, the knowledge that she was sharing power with a child not of pure royal blood, as well as the fact that she would lose this power once he matured and became pharaoh in his own right, must have been galling. For a few years, however, she accepted the situation, and served as regent. Stone carvings from the era show Hatshepsut remaining respectfully behind Thutmose III on ceremonial occasions.

But in the seventh year of her regency, approximately 1498 B.C., Hatshepsut took the throne, proclaimed herself king, and became, for all intents and purposes, sole ruler of Egypt.

How she did this, and why, is unknown. While the precise method by which Hatshepsut assumed the throne is not certain, no evidence exists of any sudden action such as a coup. Rather, as Tyldesley writes, "Hers was a gradual evolution, a carefully controlled political manoeuvre so insidious that it might not have been apparent to any but her closest contemporaries."[13]

One thing that was very clear, however, was that an event unprecedented in Egyptian history had occurred. A woman was king and

Hatshepsut claimed the throne of Egypt for herself and took the title of king. She even wore the traditional false beard of the pharaohs.

wore the double crown, symbolic of her authority over both Upper and Lower Egypt.

Hatshepsut could not have become ruler without the strong support of a close circle of advisers, religious leaders, and political friends, some of them perhaps dating back to her father's reign.

However, this was not sufficient to quell the anxiety Egyptians probably felt about having a woman on the throne. To try to reassure them, Hatshepsut had herself portrayed as a male. Not only did representations show her without breasts and wearing male clothing, but they also pictured her wearing the traditional false beard of the pharaoh. Only a few statues showed her as a woman.

She also insisted on being called "His Majesty," although sometimes the scribes, in their confusion, amended this to "His Majesty, herself."[14]

Hatshepsut knew that she needed to do more to cement her claim to the throne. Therefore, she devised a story in which she claimed that her still-revered father had handpicked her to be ruler, and she had been coregent with him during his final years on the throne.

Whether there actually was a coregency between Hatshepsut and her father is a matter that has been debated by experts. As biographer Evelyn Wells writes, "The official records are badly damaged, but it is clear that during the rest of the life of Thothmes [another way to spell Thutmose] I his daughter Hatshepsut shared the throne as his coregent and Great Queen."[15]

Others, however, feel that the coregency story was invented by Hatshepsut to secure her claim to the throne. Tyldesley writes that "there is absolutely no evidence to show that Tuthmosis I ever regarded Hatchepsut as his formal successor, or that he had the intention of passing over both his son and his grandson in order to honour his daughter."[16]

Even this story, however, was not enough to reassure Hatshepsut that Egyptians would accept a woman as their king. Thus, like many pharaohs before and after her, she reinvented history by concocting an elaborate tale in which she claimed that her real father was actually the god Amon. This meant that she was literally a child of the gods. Inscribed on the wall of her tomb was the story of this heavenly union:

> Amon took the form of the noble King Tuthmose [Thutmose] and found the queen sleeping in her room. When the pleasant odours that proceeded from him announced his presence she woke. He gave her his heart and showed himself in his godlike splendour. When he approached the queen she wept for joy at his strength and beauty and he gave her his love.[17]

Afterwards, Hatshepsut had Amon proclaim his affection for her, as well as give legitimacy to her reign, by having him say: "Welcome my sweet daughter, my favorite, the key of Upper and Lower Egypt, the moat-lover, Hatshepsut—thou art the king, take possession of the two lands."[18]

Through these types of propaganda, Hatshepsut managed to forestall any challenges to her right to the throne. But it must have been difficult for her to maintain the delicate balancing act between functioning as ruler and asserting that she belonged as king in the first place. All of the gossip, plotting, and deception that frequently surrounded the Egyptian throne must have seemed doubly threatening to a woman whose right to hold the crown was tenuous at best. An artist named Winifred Brunton, who painted a portrait of Hatshepsut, said that "into her portrait . . . there crept, almost without my will, a look of watchfulness, or even suspicion. . . . Amid so many enemies and spies, she must have felt perpetually insecure."[19]

Thutmose III's Reaction

One of the most extraordinary things about Hatshepsut's assumption of the throne was the reaction of her coregent, Thutmose III. Once Hatshepsut became pharaoh, Thutmose III faded into the background. Hatshepsut ruled the country.

This unique situation was delicately described by the scribes:

In order to secure her status as pharaoh, Hatshepsut claimed to be the daughter of Amon, king of the Egyptian gods.

His [Thutmose II's] son, being arisen in his place as King of the Two Lands, ruled upon the throne of the begetter, while his sister, the god's wife Hatshepsut, governed the land and the Two Lands were under her control; people worked for her, and Egypt bowed the head.[20]

A controversy still rages today over the exact relationship between Hatshepsut and Thutmose III. Some Egyptologists feel that Hatshepsut stole the crown from Thutmose, and that he fumed in the background while she wielded the power that he considered rightfully his.

Fueling this school of thought is the fact that someone tried to wipe out all traces of Hatshepsut after her reign ended by smashing her statues and monuments and erasing her figure and name from inscriptions. These scholars believe that Thutmose III did this as revenge. In *A History of Ancient Egypt*, author Nicolas

Grimal refers to the "fury" of Thutmose III against Hatshepsut, writing: "He [Thutmose III] attempted to hammer out Hatshepsut's name on all of her monuments, thus condemning her to oblivion."[21]

Others, however, dispute this portrait of the angry stepson. Initially, if Thutmose was an infant or a boy when Hatshepsut claimed the throne, there would have been little he could have done to stop his stepmother. However, as he matured, the reason why he didn't try to wrest the throne back from her becomes more obvious. The fact that Hatshepsut did not take steps against Thutmose if she thought he was seething in resentment against her seems to suggest their relationship was not competitive. As Tyldesley writes,

Hatchepsut's treatment of the young Tuthmosis III indicates that she never regarded his existence as a serious problem even though, as an intelligent woman, she must have realized that every passing year would strengthen his claim to rule alone. She never attempted to establish a solo reign, and instead of hiding the boy-king away or even having him killed, she was careful to accord him all the respect due to a fellow monarch.[22]

When he finally did assume the throne on his own, Thutmose III became one of the greatest pharaohs in Egyptian history, a fearless warrior whose relentless string of military victories has earned him the title "the Napoléon of Egypt." It seems unlikely that such a ferocious fighter would merely stew in impotent silence while someone else sat on his throne. In addition, the attacks on Hatshepsut's monuments and memory came near the end of Thutmose III's solo reign. If his hatred of Hatshepsut was so great, it is probable that Thutmose would have begun a campaign of eradication much earlier.

The Reign of Hatshepsut

Whatever trepidations Hatshepsut felt once she assumed the throne, they did not affect her ability to govern. Her approximately twenty-year reign is given high marks by Egyptologists because she kept the country both prosperous and peaceful.

Although Hatshepsut waged military campaigns against the Ethiopians and possibly other kingdoms or peoples, they seem to be defensive in nature and not concerned with empire building. Instead of military conquests, she focused on domestic matters such

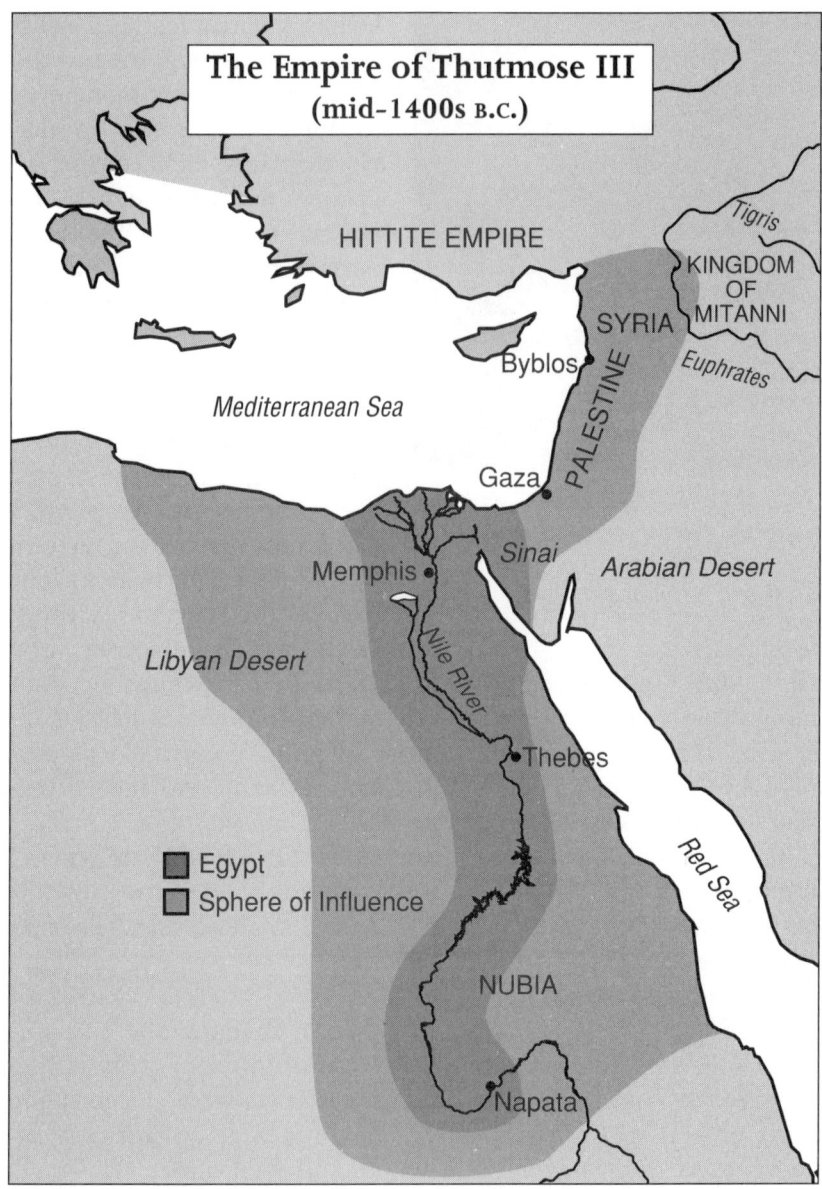

The Empire of Thutmose III
(mid-1400s B.C.)

HITTITE EMPIRE

KINGDOM OF MITANNI

Tigris

SYRIA

Euphrates

Byblos

PALESTINE

Mediterranean Sea

Gaza

Memphis

Sinai

Arabian Desert

Libyan Desert

Nile River

Thebes

Red Sea

Egypt
Sphere of Influence

NUBIA

Napata

as rebuilding old temples and constructing new ones as well as developing new trading routes and partners for Egypt.

Her lack of interest in military affairs might well have stemmed from her traditional, conservative view that a pharaoh's duty was to keep Egypt safe within its territorial boundaries, raise monuments to the gods, enrich the land through trade, and restrict contact with the outside world.

This policy was in keeping with the pharoahs of the Twelfth

Dynasty, which featured a succession of strong rulers who brought prosperity by tending to Egypt's domestic affairs. Hatshepsut's lack of foreign intrigue and emphasis on domestic matters might have been a conscious attempt to emulate the Twelfth Dynasty.

Another reason exists why Hatshepsut concentrated on domestic issues. To some Egyptians, having a female pharaoh might have seemed like an offense against *maat*, a word meaning "a universe in which everything was in harmony." A period without *maat* meant disorder and chaos, and was dreaded by all Egyptians. By following a vigorous domestic policy that emphasized internal improvements and increased trading opportunities for Egyptian goods, Hatshepsut may have been trying to demonstrate that *maat* was indeed present in the country, despite its gender-bending pharaoh.

Though there was some military activity during her reign, Hatshepsut concentrated mostly on domestic affairs such as building and trade.

Only a few accounts of Hatsheput's trade expeditions remain. One that is covered in detail is an expedition to Punt (possibly the eastern part of modern-day Sudan or the Somalia coast). The trip's primary purpose was to obtain incense, which was one of Punt's chief products.

The Egyptians were greeted by the local chieftain and his enormously overweight wife; her obesity was a source of great amusement to the visitors. The Egyptians traded necklaces, daggers, and other objects with their hosts in return for large quantities of incense (myrrh) trees, ivory, rare wood, and even cattle.

Hatshepsut was so pleased by the results of the expedition that she had it portrayed in scenes on the walls of her tomb. What is unique is that, instead of static images, the scenes are like little stories, and they often have titles. The title "Watch Your Step!" is inscribed over a picture of sailors loading goods into a ship. There is even some tongue-in-cheek humor: "The Ass Which Carries His Wife" is the title of a scene showing a small donkey trotting behind the chief's obese wife.

Hatshepsut spoke about the importance of these missions and

their effect on the country:

> Roshawet [Sinai] and Iuu [an unknown land] have not remained hidden from my august person, and Punt overflows for me on the fields, its trees bearing fresh myrrh. The roads that were blocked on both sides are now trodden. My army, which was unequipped, has become possessed of riches since I arose as king.[23]

Along with an aggressive trading policy, Hatshepsut channeled her energies into a vigorous building program, aided by her chief architect, Senenmut. He was of humble birth and first became known as an army scribe. Upon entering Hatshepsut's service, Senenmut quickly rose to a position of prominence unmatched in her administration. The holder of more than eighty titles, Senenmut was the pharaoh's chief adviser, builder, friend, and possibly even lover.

Hatshepsut repaired the many temples damaged during the Hyksos era. She also raised two enormous obelisks, both about one hundred feet tall, of red granite at Karnak. In an engineering feat that is still marveled at today, Senenmut and his workers, using just stone tools, quarried both 350-ton obelisks and brought them to Thebes via the Nile in just seven months. Once there, army and navy troops pulled the giant obelisks to the temple.

Then, in another remarkable engineering effort, the Egyptians raised both obelisks perfectly upright, using nothing more than

Hatshepsut, aided by her chief architect Senenmut, repaired the damage the Hyksos occupation caused to many of Egypt's temples, including the temple at Karnak.

Hatshepsut's tomb at Deir el-Bahri is one of the greatest architectural feats accomplished by Senenmut during her reign.

ropes, manpower, and leverage. Both obelisks were sheathed in electrum, a pale-yellow alloy of gold and silver, so that they literally glowed when struck by sunlight. In her dedication speech, Hatshepsut noted that their glow could be seen on both sides of the river.

An even more impressive achievement, however, was Hatshepsut's tomb at Deir el-Bahri. Often called the most beautiful temple in Egypt, Deir el-Bahri sits against the harsh, worn mountains of western Thebes. It is near the temple of Mentuhotep I, the warrior king who reunited Egypt after the First Intermediate Period. The temple's golden white limestone buildings, spread out over 328 feet with their clear, straight lines, are strikingly set off by the craggy brown cliffs behind them.

Senenmut actually began the temple in the midst of cultivated land, building a gently sloping causeway lined with sacred trees reaching all the way to the foot of the barren mountains. There he built a series of three terraces; slightly inclined ramps led to each level. Each terrace was lined with porticos, which were supported with fluted columns. An avenue of sphinxes led to the lower terrace. Trees and other greenery dotted the entrance to the temple.

Inside the temple were sanctuaries, a great hall filled with columns, and the royal funerary chapel. The walls were covered with scenes from Hatshepsut's reign.

Like her trading policies, Hatshepsut emphasized domestic building projects to show the Egyptian people that the land was prosperous and the gods were happy despite the presence of a female on the pharaoh's throne. All was right with the world, as Hatshepsut points out:

> I have done these things by the device of my heart. I have never slumbered as one forgetful, but have made strong what was decayed. I have raised up what was dismembered, even from the first time when the Asiatics [the Hyksos] were in Avaris of the North Land, with roving hordes in the midst of them overthrowing what had been made; they ruled without Re. . . . I have banished the abominations of the gods, and the earth has removed their footprints.[24]

Unfortunately, stilted inscriptions such as this are virtually the only clues to Hatshepsut's personality. As Joyce Tyldesley writes,

> The private woman—Hatchepsut as daughter, wife and mother—has been far more difficult to reach as we are lacking almost all the intimate details which can help a historical character come alive to the modern reader. Hatchepsut lived in a literate age, but belonged to a society which did not believe in keeping personal written records.[25]

The Mystery of Hatshepsut's Fate

For more than twenty years, Hatshepsut ruled Egypt in a firm, intelligent manner: fighting only when she had to, promoting prosperity through trade, and constructing some of the most beautiful and unique structures ever seen in the country. She compiled an impressive record of accomplishment. "My command stands firm like the mountains, and the sun's disk shines and spreads rays over the titulary of my august person, and my falcon rises high above the kingly banner unto all eternity,"[26] reads one of her inscriptions.

Then, around 1482 B.C., she was gone. In her place was Thutmose III, ready to begin his reign. Although theories about Hatshepsut's fate range from assassination to death by illness, it is likely that, as a woman between thirty-five and fifty-five years of age, she simply died of natural causes.

Clearly, Hatshepsut had been proud of her accomplishments and had been eager for the judgment of history, as evidenced by this inscription: "Now my heart turns this way and that, as I think what the people will say. Those who shall see my monuments in years to come, and who shall speak of what I have done."[27]

Hatshepsut's mummy has never been found. If it ever is, perhaps more of the mysteries of this "first great woman in history" will be solved.

CHAPTER 3

Akhenaten: Heretic or Visionary?

For no other pharaoh is expert opinion so divided as it is for Amenhotep IV, who changed his name to Akhenaten. Some Egyptologists feel that this New Kingdom pharaoh was a bold religious visionary whose attempt to change Egypt's religious orientation from worshiping many gods (polytheism) to worshiping just one (monotheism) was centuries ahead of its time. Others say he was a political reformer who tried to curb the power of the priesthood by lessening the influence of their gods. Another school of thought is that he was a weak, delusional man, whose slavish devotion to a single god emanating from the sun betrayed the workings of an unbalanced mind.

The Reign of Amenhotep III

Amenhotep IV (he did not change his name to Akhenaten until he became pharaoh) was born around 1386 B.C. His father was Pharaoh Amenhotep III of the Eighteenth Dynasty and his mother was Queen Tiy.

During Amenhotep III's reign, Egypt was the richest and most powerful nation in the ancient world. Tribute from conquered lands flooded into Egypt, and the country prospered as never before. Other monarchs took Egypt's riches for granted, as one ruler who was friendly with Egypt wrote to the king: "Send gold, quickly, in very great quantities, so that I may finish a work I am undertaking; for gold is as dust in the land of my brother."[28]

Other nations were so cowed by Egypt's military might that it was no longer necessary for the pharaoh to go on even minor campaigns to demonstrate the awesome power of his army. Amenhotep was able to remain in Thebes, in the comfort and splendor of his royal court, and not worry that an uprising in some distant land would force him into battle.

With the threat of war virtually nonexistent, Amenhotep was free to focus his energies elsewhere. Hunting was one of his favorite pastimes. He was once said to have shot over one hundred lions single-handedly. He also liked printing accounts of his activities onto what are today called "historical scarabs" (beetle-shaped plaques) and distributing them throughout the kingdom.

However, Amenhotep's primary interest lay in building. He built and repaired temples, shrines, statues, palaces, and numerous other structures throughout Egypt. By the second year of his reign, the pharaoh's frenetic campaign already needed new sources of raw materials. An inscription talks about the pharaoh opening new quarry chambers so that more limestone could be extracted for building purposes.

Not only did Amenhotep have the time to devote to building, he also had the resources, thanks to Egypt's wealth. In just one temple, Egyptian builders used two and a half tons of gold.

Thus, Amenhotep IV grew up in a relaxed, opulent lifestyle. Little is known about his early life; this is mainly because, unlike his four sisters and one brother, he was not depicted on the monuments and other structures his father built. It is almost as if he did not exist at all.

No one knows why Amenhotep is absent. Some speculate that he was deliberately kept in the background because of a glandular ailment called Frohlich's syndrome, which distorted his features.

When Akhenaten became pharaoh, Egypt was the wealthiest nation in the world. With plenty of time and resources at their disposal, the pharaohs often undertook massive building projects.

Though the primary god of the Egyptians was Amon, Akhenaten (pictured) began to worship the god Aten. Some feel he did this to lessen the power of the priests of Amon.

This condition gave the young man an elongated skull, fleshy lips, slanting eyes, lengthened earlobes, a prominent jaw, a potbelly, and spindly legs. (However, since another symptom of this condition is infertility, and Amenhotep would go on to father at least six daughters, such a diagnosis is improbable.)

Since young Amenhotep was not pictured on the monuments and in other family scenes, it is unlikely that he participated with his family in religious ceremonies held in the temples. He probably remained behind at the royal court.

During the later years of his reign, Amenhotep III and his family lived in Thebes, which had become the religious center of Egypt. To seek favor with the gods, each pharaoh built temples honoring the deities at Karnak, the religious heart of Thebes. As each pharaoh added to Karnak, it became a virtual maze of temples, sprawling over one hundred acres. Offerings of bread, wine, gold, linens, land, and other valuables flowed into the temples to thank the gods for blessing Egypt with power and prosperity.

As the temples grew more wealthy, the influence of the priests increased accordingly. The most powerful was the high priest of Amon, the supreme god of Egypt. The combination of religious significance and enormous wealth made him as important as the pharaoh.

Possibly to diminish the priests' power, Amenhotep quietly embraced a secondary god called the Aten (sometimes spelled Aton). The Aten was the actual physical disk of the sun. Amenhotep built a temple to the Aten in the royal precinct of Memphis, which was the administrative center of Egypt. He also constructed a small Aten temple in Thebes and worshiped the Aten along with the other gods.

In the final years of his reign, Amenhotep III was an old, overweight man with abscessed teeth that must have caused him considerable pain. Possibly because of his health, he needed help running the country. Since his other son had died, the pharaoh named Amenhotep IV coregent. When his father died, the odd-looking youngster became the leader of the ancient world's most powerful country.

Embracing the Aten

By now Amenhotep IV had married Nefertiti, a slim, attractive woman whose name means "the beautiful woman has come." More than any other Egyptian queen, Nefertiti was a full partner with her husband. She appeared on more statues and inscriptions than he did, and she sometimes was shown discharging duties normally performed by the pharaoh. For instance, one carving shows her grabbing prisoners by the hair and striking them with a mace—a pose previously only assumed by the pharaoh to show him dispatching the country's enemies.

Amenhotep's own words display his obvious feelings for Nefertiti:

Akhenaten's wife, Nefertiti, was considered to be his equal in many respects. She is often depicted carrying out the duties of the pharaoh.

The Hereditary Princess, Great of Favor, Mistress of Happiness, Gay with the two feathers, at hearing whose voice one rejoices, Soothing the heart of the king at home, pleased with all that is said, the Great and Beloved Wife of the King, Lady of the Two Lands, Neferu-aten Nefertiti, living forever.[29]

If the Egyptians thought that life under Amenhotep IV would be the same as it had been under his father, they soon learned otherwise.

One of the most radical changes occurred in Egyptian art. For centuries, Egyptian art had been rigid and formula-driven. Pharaohs, no matter whether they were short, tall, fat, or skinny, had always been portrayed as individuals with perfect physiques, without the hint of physical imperfection. The same held true for

Akhenaten was the first pharaoh to be portrayed in a realistic manner by the Egyptian artists. The previous pharaohs were always depicted as perfect physical specimens.

their families. In addition, pharaohs were always depicted as performing noble tasks, such as crushing Egypt's enemies in battle. The Amarna style of Amenhotep's reign was in complete contrast to this; suddenly, Egyptians were viewing portraits of their pharaoh that not only displayed imperfections but seemed intent on exaggerating them. The pharaoh and his family were also depicted in less-than-heroic settings.

Amenhotep was shown with elongated fingers and toes, wide hips, protruding belly, feminine breasts, and a long, thin face. The pharaoh's family, Nefertiti and his six daughters, were shown with elongated heads and narrow, slanted eyes.

The pharaoh's shape was so curiously drawn, in fact, that when his tomb was rediscovered in the 1880s, researchers who looked at portraits of the royal couple at first thought that they were gazing upon two women.

The pharaoh was depicted enjoying everyday family activities such as standing arm-in-arm with Nefertiti, and watching his children frolic in the garden.

These changes, however, were only a prelude to those of a more profound nature that occurred in Egyptian religion.

Early in his reign Amenhotep declared that Egypt's gods had failed and/or ceased to exist. He also began to enlarge and beautify the Aten temple in Thebes. However, since he continued to worship the traditional gods, at first no radical changes occurred.

Soon, however, Amenhotep issued decrees that affected the worship of the god Aten: Amenhotep ordered that the name of the district in Thebes where the Aten temple was located be changed to "the Brightness of Aten the Great." He also declared that

Thebes, the city of Amon, be renamed "the City of the Brightness of Aten."

A New City

But the biggest surprise came in the fifth year of his reign. After a lengthy absence from Thebes, Amenhotep returned to announce that he planned to build a new city, nearly two hundred miles to the north, dedicated solely to the Aten. The city was to be called Akhetaten, which means "the horizon of the Aten." (Today it is called Tell el-Amarna.)

The pharaoh himself chose the new city's location. While traveling through a desolate stretch of desert, he observed that when the sun rose on the horizon, it seemed to rest in a notch in the mountains. The sun resting in a mountain notch is also the hieroglyphical sign for horizon. Amenhotep considered this a sign from the Aten to build in that spot. As Cyril Aldred said, "It was solely the Aten who had directed him to this virgin site."[30]

Initially, the impact of Amenhotep's changes was confined to Thebes. Biographer Donald B. Redford writes that outside of Thebes, the traditional gods were still worshiped during the first years of the pharaoh's reign.

The announcement of Amenhotep's new city, however, must have stunned many Egyptians. The pharaoh was replacing the city that had been the religious heart of Egypt in favor of a new site

Akhenaten decided to shift the religious center of Egypt from Thebes to a new city that was to be built in the middle of the desert. This new city was called Akhetaten.

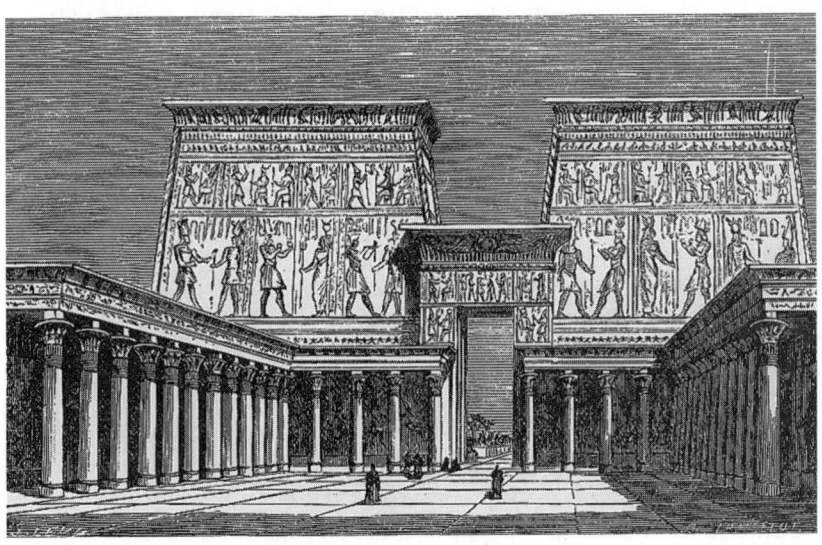

far off in the desert. It would be like the Roman Catholic Church moving from Rome to a brand new town in the Sahara. A further blow to Thebes came when Amenhotep revealed that he was leaving Thebes to live in Akhetaten. The new city was going to be both the religious and governmental center of the country.

As his new city rose in the desert, the king changed his name from Amenhotep (meaning "Amon is satisfied") to Akhenaten ("effective for the sun-Disk"). Nefertiti changed her name to Neferneferuaten ("fair is the beauty of the aten"). The pharaoh also ordered people with names compounded with the word *Amon* to change them. Then the pharaoh closed the temples of the traditional gods. An army of officials was dispatched to remove Amon and the other gods from statues, buildings, and temples.

With these sweeping and radical actions, Akhenaten made it clear that there was just one god, and it was the Aten. No others were permitted. To emphasize this, after the fifth year of Akhenaten's reign, the plural word *gods* was never used again while he was pharaoh, and it was even removed from places where it appeared.

There are several theories as to why Akhenaten changed the way Egyptians had worshiped for two thousand years. One is that, because he never participated in the religious ceremonies with his family, he never felt loyalty or devotion to the old gods. Thus, it was easy for him to discard them in favor of the (then-secondary) god, the Aten.

Another possibility is that he was trying to curb the power of the priests, particularly those devoted to Amon. By closing the temples, Akhenaten turned off the tap of offerings that were the foundation of the priesthood's power. Now these riches went to Akhetaten instead.

Some even think Akhenaten was a religious visionary—a man who instituted the worship of one god centuries before Christianity began. Still others feel that he was ill and that his actions stemmed from insanity or some other affliction.

Whatever his reasons, Akhenaten's actions sent repercussions throughout Egypt. Priests, of course, were furious; they had been literally thrown out of their jobs. Weeds grew in the courtyards of the Karnak temples, and stray dogs scavenged for food where priests had once led illustrious processions in honor of the gods.

It was not only priests who were upset with the pharaoh, however. Religion was an important industry in Egypt; anyone whose livelihood depended on the gods, such as wood carvers, stonecutters, amulet makers, and others who produced statues and figures of the gods, suddenly found themselves without a trade.

The Egyptian people must have been bewildered and possibly even frightened by this great upheaval in their lives. The old gods had led Egypt to the pinnacle of power in the ancient world; now they were all rejected.

Worshiping the Aten was a big change for Egyptians. As Akhenaten made clear, only he was the representative of the Aten: "There is none who knows thee save my son Akhenaten. Thou hast made him wise in my plans and my power."[31]

The only way for people to worship the Aten was to worship the pharaoh. For thousands of years Egyptians had worshiped gods they could represent via statues, amulets, and other figures, and these gods possessed human bodies with animal heads. But the Aten was an abstraction—a disk with sunlight coming down from it.

Akhenaten was the first pharaoh in Egyptian art to be depicted performing everyday tasks, such as praying with his family (pictured).

Recently, new findings have suggested that some Egyptians continued to invoke their previous religious ways. Excavations at Akhetaten have uncovered prayers to Amon, meaning that even those who built and lived in the new city dedicated to the Aten were still worshiping the old gods.

But if Akhenaten knew about the ambivalent feelings of some of his people, he ignored them. In the eighth year of his reign, the pharaoh and his royal court left Thebes for Akhetaten.

New City, New Problems

Once there, Akhenaten was like a child with a new toy. Often during the first few years the pharaoh appeared in public riding in his chariot and overseeing the construction of a new building or temple. Neferneferuaten frequently accompanied him, along with one or more of his daughters. Everywhere there was activity, as workers strove to raise a city from the desolate desert. By the ninth year of Akhenaten's reign, many of Akhetaten's major buildings were either done or nearing completion.

When he was not checking on his city's progress, the pharaoh was worshiping his god and contemplating the deeper meaning of the Aten. Eventually Akhenaten composed an epic poem called *Hymn to the Aten*. The poem revealed the passion of his conviction:

> Splendid you rise in heaven's lightland, O living Aten, creator of life! When you have dawned in eastern highland, You fill every land with your beauty. You are beauteous, great, radiant, High over every land.[32]

But the more time the pharaoh devoted to the Aten, the less he spent on the affairs of Egypt. Because it had been years since the great Egyptian army fought in battle, the memory of its might had faded. Other nations began to boldly encroach upon Egyptian territory. In the north the powerful Hittites from Syria swallowed up small kingdoms that thought Egypt would protect them. Frantic monarchs begged Akhenaten for help. "They say that the king my lord will not march out," wrote Akizzi, ruler of Qatanum, to Akhenaten. "So let my lord dispatch archers, and let them come."[33]

But no one came. As word spread of Akhenaten's aversion to war, other areas, such as Palestine, were attacked by outside forces. The pharaoh received more pleas: "Abdashirta is marching with his brethren. March against him and smite him!"[34] urged one ruler.

While Akhenaten devoted countless hours to worshiping Aten, the once mighty Egyptian army was falling into disarray. Egypt's enemies began to boldly encroach upon its territory.

These appeals were also ignored. The Egyptian Empire was fraying at the edges, but Akhenaten either never heard these cries for help or else he did not care.

Further compounding Egypt's military woes was the fact that the army was not the mighty machine of old. Years of inactivity and being used primarily for domestic tasks, such as laboring in quarries and helping to build structures, had dulled its fighting edge. Even a dynamic military ruler would have had trouble rehabilitating the army and leading it into battle against powerful enemies. For the peaceful Akhenaten, this task was virtually impossible.

Egypt also had domestic problems. Unemployed soldiers wandered the country preying on helpless citizens. Dishonest tax collectors took advantage of a lax central government by extorting money from people. Legions of defrocked priests helped stir up trouble against the "heretic" pharaoh who had put them out of work.

Even rulers from other countries were unhappy with Akhenaten. Although the king enjoyed sitting in the sunlight provided by the Aten, others did not find it pleasant. When envoys from King Ashuruballit I of Assyria complained to their ruler about waiting in the hot sun to see the pharaoh, the king complained to Akhenaten:

Why are my messengers kept standing in the open sun? They will die in the open sun. If it does the king good to stand in the open sun, then let the king stand there and die in the open sun. Then will there be profit for the king![35]

Adding to Akhenaten's problems was a wave of death that swept over his family during the final years of his reign. Several of

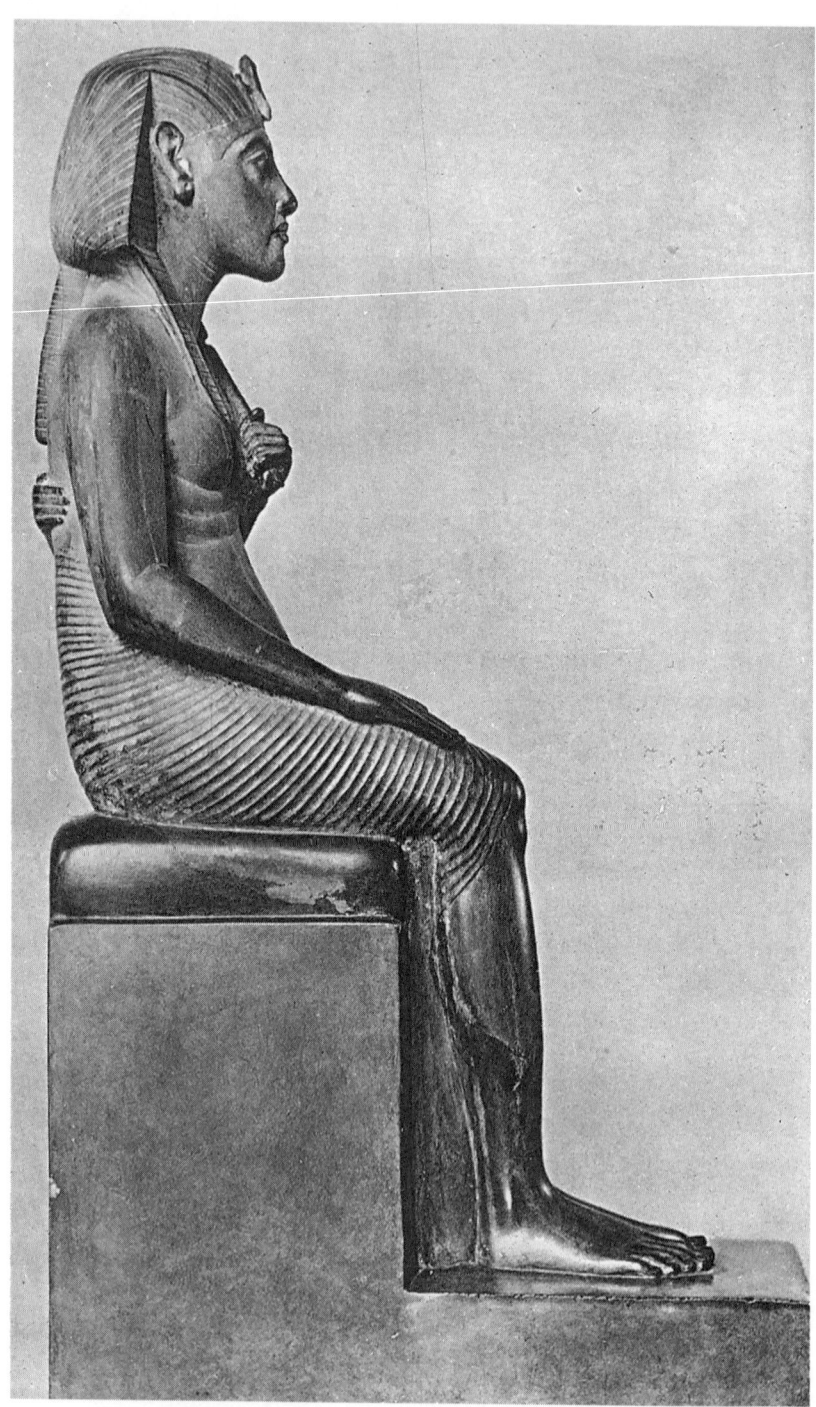

After Akhenaten's death, Egypt once again began to worship Amon and the other gods. The once major metropolis of Akhetaten was abandoned, left to be erased by the desert.

the king's daughters died as well as his mother, Queen Tiy. Neferneferuaten also disappeared in the fourteenth year of Akhenaten's reign, but no one knows if she died or was banished for some reason.

Death and Mystery

The events of Akhenaten's last few years are shrouded in mystery. Some Egyptologists believe he appointed a coregent named Smenkhkare, who may have been his younger brother. Smenkhkare was sent to Thebes, possibly to begin repairing the temples at Karnak and bring Amon and the other gods back into favor.

Akhenaten died during the seventeenth year of his reign. It is uncertain who followed him to the throne. Some believe it was Smenkhkare, while others feel that Neferneferuaten may have briefly reemerged to wear the crown before passing it on to Smenkhkare.

Smenkhkare's reign lasted only three years. Upon his death he was succeeded by a pharaoh whose name is instantly familiar to millions of people today: Tutankhamon.

Although the Aten cult did not immediately collapse with the passing of Akhenaten, his death removed the earthly foundation on which the entire movement was based. Aten worshiping was linked too closely with Akhenaten to survive after he was gone. Slowly cult members drifted back to the old ways and the traditional gods who were reinstated by Tutankhamon. The great religious experiment had failed.

Ultimately, the Aten cult was blamed for the woes afflicting Egypt. Akhetaten was ordered abandoned, and the desert sands eventually covered up this once-major metropolis. Evidence of its existence remained hidden for thousands of years.

Akhenaten suffered a similar fate. His name and likeness were removed throughout Egypt, his statues toppled, and his temples dismantled. Priestly scribes omitted Akhenaten's name from their chronological lists of Egypt's kings and tried never to utter his name. When it was impossible to avoid speaking about him, chroniclers used enigmatic phrases such as "the reign of that damned one."[36] Like his city, Akhenaten remained hidden for centuries.

Although details of his reign have now been uncovered (the mummies of both Akhenaten and Neferneferuaten have never been found, however), questions persist about Akhenaten and his actions. The riddle of why he did what he did remains one of the most intriguing in the vast history of ancient Egypt.

CHAPTER 4

Tutankhamon: Egypt's Most Famous Pharaoh

In life he was a minor pharaoh. His reign during Egypt's Eighteenth Dynasty was short and insignificant. When he died at age eighteen, he was buried with pomp and ceremony, and the country moved on. Never in their wildest dreams could Egyptians have imagined that of all the kings in their long and glorious history, the name of this young boy would be the one to live on thousands of years into the future. For the ancient Egyptians, who fervently believed in an afterlife, it is fitting that the legacy of Tutankhamon has been forged in death, not life.

Although Tutankhamon's reign was relatively insignificant, he has become the most recognizable of Egypt's pharaohs.

A Boy Becomes King

When Tutankhamon assumed the throne of Egypt after Smenkhkare's death, around 1333 B.C., he was just nine years old. Although his parentage is unknown, some experts believe his father was Amenhotep III, but the identity of his mother remains unknown. This would make Tutankhamon Akhenaten's half brother. Others, however, feel that Queen Tiy, Amenhotep's royal wife, was his mother, and that Akhenaten was his biological brother.

At birth he was called Tutankhaten (meaning "living image of the Aten"), with the suffix -*aten* illustrating the influence of the Aten religious cult. While growing up, Tutankhaten was indoctrinated into the sun-disk religion. However, the fact that his name was changed to Tutankhamon ("living image of Amon") when he became pharaoh indicates that the old religious ways were coming back into favor. Another clue that the Aten cult was receding was that the coronation services were held in the former religious center of Thebes and not Akhenaten's city of Akhetaten.

Although just a boy when he became king of Egypt, Tutankhamon married the royal princess Ankhesenamen (whose name had been changed from Ankhesenpaaten, which again illustrates how the Aten cult had fallen out of favor).

Repairing the Damage

Pressing problems immediately faced young Tutankhamon. Egypt was in turmoil, thanks mainly to Akhenaten's fixation on the Aten cult to the exclusion of his other duties. Problems both at home and abroad beset the kingdom; the days of Amenhotep III, when no foreign enemy dared risk Egypt's might and the country was awash in wealth, were long gone.

Tutankhamon issued an edict, putting into words what many Egyptians thought: Abandoning the traditional gods was the reason the country was in trouble. According to the edict,

> Now His Majesty appeared as king at a time when the temples of gods and goddess from Elephantine as far as the Delta marshes had fallen into ruin, and their shrines become dilapidated. They had turned into mounds overgrown with [weeds], and it seemed that their sanctuaries had never existed: their *enceintes* were [crisscrossed] with footpaths. This land had been struck by catastrophe: the gods had turned their backs upon it. If [ever] the army was dispatched to the Levant to extend the borders of Egypt, they had no success. If [ever] one prayed to a god to ask something of him, he never would come at all; if [ever] one supplicated any goddess likewise, she would never come at all. Their hearts were weakened in their bodies, [for] they had destroyed what had been made.[37]

Slowly the religious machinery that had grown rusty from years of inactivity during Akhenaten's reign began to operate again. To regain favor with the gods, the pharaoh ordered new temples built (including one in the image of Amon, which would be the largest ever made), established new priesthoods, beefed up the ranks of existing religious orders, and resumed making offerings to the temples. Tutankhamon initiated so much activity in Thebes that it was said he had reestablished the city's prominence.

When Tutankhamon came to power, he made an active effort to move Egypt away from the changes instituted by Akhenaten. Egyptian art once again portrayed the pharaoh as a perfect being leading military expeditions and hunts.

An inscribed tablet described Tutankhamon's actions:

> I found the temple in ruins, the holy places destroyed and the courtyards overgrown with weeds. I restored the shrines and the temples and gave them jewels. I made pictures of the gods out of gold and amber, decorated with lapis lazuli and precious stones.[38]

In another act to restore traditional ways, artists portrayed Tutankhamon hunting and leading military campaigns, just like the kings of old. There were no more scenes of the pharaoh and his family relaxing in the garden, as were common during Akhenaten's time. Art styles reverted back to what they had been before the Amarna period, showing the pharaoh and his family as perfect individuals, without the sagging belly, drooping shoulders, and other physical imperfections that were depicted during Ahkenaten's reign.

Tutankhamon also tried to shake Egypt out of its military lethargy. Campaigns were mounted against the Nubians and other enemies in Africa, and Egypt's tenuous hold on Palestine and Lebanon was reinforced. However, these were campaigns of consolidation rather than conquest.

The Return of Amon

Since Tutankhamon was a youth during much of his reign, he received advice about foreign and domestic policy, religious restoration, military campaigns, and other governmental matters. Two of his most trusted advisers were his vizier, Ay, and Horemheb, a military general. Egyptologists believe Horemheb guided the country's return to Amon and the traditional gods.

Amon's resurgence did not immediately initiate a widespread attack on followers of the Aten cult. No temples were closed, no inscriptions wiped out, and no cult leaders persecuted. After all, Tutankhamon had been raised as a member of the Aten cult; it was still a religion he was close to, even though it had fallen out of favor. Instead of openly repudiating the Aten, the pharaoh simply let it be known through his words and actions that the Aten was *not* the sole god; there were other gods also, and people were permitted and even encouraged to worship them. Gradually the Aten slipped back into the secondary role in Egyptian life that it had occupied before Akhenaten's reign.

A Move to Thebes

Because the Aten was no longer the primary god, it was inappropriate for the pharaoh to continue living in Akhetaten. Sometime during the third or fourth year of his reign, Tutankhamon left Akhetaten for Thebes. It is unlikely that he ever again visited Akhenaten's city, which slowly slipped into disrepair and was finally abandoned.

Between ages fifteen and eighteen, Tutankhamon demonstrated that the teachings of Ay, Horemheb, and others were not in vain. He was developing political skills, learning how to balance influences, strengthen alliances, and keep adversaries at bay. This was demonstrated by how he played on the anxieties of Burnaburiash, king of Karaduniash (Babylonia), concerning the possibility of Egypt's strengthening ties with Burnaburiash's vassals, the Assyrians.

Burnaburiash was worried that the Assyrians would rebel against his authority. Tutankhamon fanned the flames of these fears by accepting an Assyrian trade delegation to his court. At the

Though he was young and inexperienced, seasoned advisers surrounded Tutankhamon. They taught him the art of diplomacy and how to deal with enemies.

same time, he delayed sending Burnaburiash some gifts that he had requested. The Babylonian king, fearful that Egypt was emboldening the Assyrians by these acts of friendship, wrote an anxious letter to Tutankhamon. Part of the letter reads:

> Now [concerning] the Assyrians, my vassals, I have written nothing to thee as they claim. Why have they gone to thy country? If thou lovest me, they must not [be allowed to] buy anything at all, let them return here empty-handed![39]

At the end of the letter, anxious to remain in Tutankhamon's good graces, Burnaburiash sent him a gift of horses and lapis lazuli.

Even thousands of years ago it was an old diplomatic trick to balance influences, divide adversaries, and strengthen alliances. By acting friendly toward the Assyrians, Tutankhamon was not only driving a bigger wedge between them and Burnaburiash but also tempering Babylonia's influence with Egypt and keeping the worried Burnaburiash as an ally eager to demonstrate his loyalty by giving the king gifts. The young king was learning how to negotiate the tricky landscape of diplomacy.

Unfortunately, his education was abruptly halted. Tutankhamon died at age eighteen.

The Mystery of Tutankhamon's Death

The cause of the young pharaoh's death is difficult to determine. According to Egyptologist Cyril Aldred, an examination of Tutankhamon's mummy revealed a wound, possibly from an arrow, that penetrated the king's skull near his left ear. After the injury Tutankhamon's head was shaved, which was standard procedure by Egyptian doctors in dealing with this type of wound. The king lived long enough to regrow a short stubble of hair on his head. At his death the slightly built Tutankhamon was approximately five feet five inches tall.

The nature of Tutankhamon's injury has led to speculation that he was murdered, although no evidence has been found to corroborate this theory. While it is possible that the wound could have been sustained during an assassination attempt, it also could have resulted from a hunting accident or from battle.

Further compounding the intrigue of the king's death is the discovery by autopsies and X rays of a small sliver of bone within the upper cranial cavity. It seems likely that this occurred because of a blow but again, what type of blow, and the manner in which it was inflicted, are unknown.

According to Hittite accounts, Tutankhamon's death caused great distress among Egyptians. Perhaps this was simply a response to the loss of their leader, or maybe it was genuine grief at the death of a monarch apparently poised to lead Egypt back to prosperity.

Due to his youth and brief reign, it is difficult for Egyptologists to rate Tutankhamon. Many consider him a minor pharaoh.

The Struggle to Succeed Tutankhamon

Because Tutankhamon left no heirs (his only child died young), there was a three-way competition to succeed him on the throne: Ankhesenamen, his wife; Ay, the aged vizier; and Horemheb, the military man. Although Ay was named pharaoh, Ankhesenamen tried desperately to regain the power she lost when her husband died.

The young queen, who had clutched the body of Tutankhamon so tightly during the burial service that some of the ashes she threw on herself in mourning clung to his shroud, wrote a secret letter to the Hittite king Suppiluliumas. In the letter Ankhesenamen begged the king to send one of his sons to Egypt for her to marry so that he would become pharaoh.

Since the two countries were enemies, Suppiluliumas was suspicious of the offer. However, after receiving a favorable report from an envoy he sent to investigate the situation, and also receiving a second letter from Ankhesenamen, the Hittite king dispatched his son Zidanza to Egypt for her to marry.

Unfortunately, Ankhesenamen's intrigues became known to others. The moment Zidanza set foot on Egyptian soil he was murdered by, according to the Hittites, "the men and horses of Egypt."[40] Young Ankhesenamen was forced to marry Ay, and thereafter disappeared from Egyptian chronicles. Certain that he

Tutankhamon's wife, Ankhesenamen, was involved in a struggle for power with her husband's advisers, Ay and Horemheb, after the young pharaoh's untimely demise. Ay was named pharaoh.

had been tricked, the furious Suppiluliumas attacked Egyptian possessions in the northern part of the empire.

Because of his advanced age, Ay's reign as pharaoh lasted just four years. He was succeeded as king by Horemheb, who initiated a full-scale campaign to eradicate all traces of Akhenaten and the Aten cult.

All this, of course, occurred after Tutankhamon was laid to rest. Some experts believe that, because of the pharaoh's sudden death, his royal tomb had not yet been completed. Thus, the small tomb he was buried in, the one that would ultimately become famous throughout the world, was actually meant for an Egyptian high official and not for a pharaoh.

Little did anyone suspect that, after sealing the door to the tiny tomb, the next time it was opened it would cause a worldwide sensation.

Tutankhamon Rediscovered

On November 4, 1922, British archaeologist Howard Carter rode his mule out to the site of a recent excavation he had begun in the Valley of the Kings. For six years Carter had stuck doggedly to his belief that the tomb of an obscure pharaoh named Tutankhamon was in the valley somewhere, waiting to be found.

He had scant evidence to go on—just some fragments of artifacts, floral wreaths, and shards of food and wine jars, some of which bore Tutankhamon's royal seal. These were found by American explorer Theodore Davis, who proclaimed that he had found the tomb. Carter, however, almost alone among his colleagues, rejected Davis's contention and launched his own search for the tomb.

But all of his efforts turned up nothing, and the fruitless expenditure of time and money had exhausted the patience of Carter's patron, Great Britain's earl of Carnarvon. Desperate, Carter asked Carnarvon to finance one final dig in a small area just below the tomb of Ramses VI. Carnarvon reluctantly agreed, and Carter launched his last-ditch effort to find a tomb that almost no one thought existed on November 1, 1922.

Arriving on his mule at the digging site on November 4, Carter was greeted by the excited cries of his foreman: "Sir, we hit a step hewn into the rock below the foundation of the first hut!"[41]

By the next day it was obvious that a tomb had been found. Fortunately, it appeared not to have been plundered by grave robbers seeking valuables, as was the fate of so many other tombs in the Valley of the Kings.

Carter sent a telegram to the earl of Carnarvon informing him of the discovery, and he then waited for his patron to arrive in Egypt so that he could be on hand to witness the opening of this spectacular find.

Finally on November 26, 1922, with Carnarvon and others waiting eagerly behind him, Carter made a small hole in the door to the tomb and, with the aid of a candle, peered inside. As Carter later wrote:

> At first I could see nothing, the hot air escaping from the chamber causing the candle flame to flicker, but presently, as my eyes grew accustomed to the light, details of the room within emerged slowly from the mist, strange animals, statues, and gold—everywhere the glint of gold.
> "Can you see anything?" asked Carnarvon excitedly.
> "Yes," [replied Carter,] "wonderful things."[42]

When the aged Ay died after a brief reign of four years, Tutankhamon's military adviser, Horemheb (pictured here on a wall of his tomb with the Egyptian god Horus), succeeded him as pharaoh.

Until archaeologist Howard Carter (middle) uncovered it on November 4, 1922, Tutankhamon's tomb had lain undisturbed for thirty-two hundred years. It is the only royal tomb that has been found virtually intact.

What he saw had not been seen by human eyes for over thirty-two hundred years. It was indeed the tomb of Tutankhamon, and it was the first sepulcher in the Valley of the Kings that was found virtually intact (a distinction it still retains).

Ironically, Carter had been close to the tomb several times before but had missed it. "Twice before," he said, "I had come within two yards of that first stone step."[43]

The discovery of Tutankhamon's tomb caused a worldwide sensation. Newspapers carried extensive stories about the find, and overnight Carter and Carnarvon became famous. People flocked to Egypt to view Tutankhamon's tomb firsthand.

It took the meticulous Carter eight years to remove, catalog, and restore the more than two thousand objects found in the tomb. Among these were furnishings, such as a cedarwood chest and a throne; objects from everyday life, such as an alabaster vase and royal daggers; and numerous statues representing the various Egyptian gods.

The greatest find, however, was the pharaoh's mummy itself, still encased in its original series of interlocking cases and coffins. The solid gold innermost coffin weighed 242 pounds and was studded with enamel inlays and colored stones. It depicted Tutankhamon as the god Osiris holding a whip and scepter, both symbols of dominion.

The "Mummy's Curse"

The discovery of Tutankhamon's tomb spawned reports of a "mummy's curse" that brought death to everyone involved with opening the tomb. According to the story, a tablet bearing the inscription "Death will slay with his wings whoever disturbs the peace of the pharaoh" was found in the tomb. (The tablet was never photographed and is considered lost.) The first victim of the curse was supposedly Carnarvon himself, who died a few months after the tomb was opened of an infection caused by the reopening of an old wound while shaving. Other supposed victims included several people who also helped excavate Tutankhamon's tomb. While routinely dismissed by Egyptologists and other experts, the curse has been a blessing for the entertainment industry, which has produced movies, books, and television shows about it.

The discovery of Tutankhamon's tomb made the boy-king the most famous pharaoh in Egypt's long history. Despite the more important and notable reigns of Ramses II, Thutmose III, Queen Hatshepsut, and numerous others, Tutankhamon came to symbolize the glory and grandeur of ancient Egypt.

Even today the name Tutankhamon, or King Tut, is familiar to millions of people the world over, but few recognize Ramses II or Thutmose III. It is one of history's supreme ironies that young Tutankhamon, whose name was removed from public buildings and other places by his successors in an attempt to erase the record of his reign, has become the most popular pharaoh in Egyptian history while everyone else has receded into the background. Although he ruled for just nine short years, the legacy of Tutankhamon seems likely to last for centuries.

CHAPTER 5

Ramses II: Egypt's Greatest Pharaoh?

Ramses II is considered one of the greatest pharaohs in ancient Egyptian history. Even his nickname—Ramses the Great—reveals how history rates him. He was a warrior, statesman, builder, politician, and more during a reign that lasted over six decades.

What no one knows, however, is whether Ramses was as mighty as he seems or if he was just a public-relations genius.

Ramses II Becomes Pharaoh

Ramses II became pharaoh in 1279 B.C. He was the third pharaoh of the Nineteenth Dynasty in the New Kingdom.

The Eighteenth Dynasty, which led Egypt to unprecedented power in the ancient world, ended with the death of Horemheb. The Nineteenth Dynasty began with Pharaoh Ramses I, a former military commander named Paramessu who reigned for just two years. He was succeeded by his son Seti I, one of the finest warriors in Egyptian history. Although he ruled for only eleven years, Seti restored much of the empire that previous pharaohs had let slip away. His finest hour came at the walled city of Kadesh in Syria, where he defeated Egypt's archenemy, the Hittites.

Paramessu, a military commander (and Ramses II's grandfather), started the Nineteenth Dynasty as Pharaoh Ramses I.

Ramses II, son of Seti and Queen Tuya, grew up in the town of Avaris in the Nile Delta region. Like most members of the country's upper class, Ramses probably learned to read and write. To prevent any confusion about whom his successor should be, and to groom his son to be pharaoh one day, Seti made Ramses prince regent when the boy was still just a teenager.

Keenly concerned about the lines of succession and the continuation of his dynasty, Seti supplied the youthful Ramses with two royal brides and other women as well. By the time of his death, Seti had the pleasure of seeing the royal wives bear at least five sons and two daughters. In addition, the other women of Ramses' harem may have supplied another dozen or more children.

From the time he was a teenager, Ramses (pictured) was groomed by his father, Seti I, to be pharaoh.

Ramses' father also made sure that the young prince received adequate military training. In his mid-teens Ramses accompanied Seti to Libya to squash a rebellion, and he was also with his father during his victory at Kadesh. A few years later, on his own with the army for the first time, Ramses crushed a revolt in Nubia by personally leading the chariot charge that won the battle. This was a tactic that Ramses would utilize a few years later against the Hittites.

Ramses II shared the throne with his father during Seti's last years. "Crown him as king that I may see his beauty while I live with him,"[44] said Seti.

When his father died in about 1280 B.C., Ramses II became sole monarch. He knew that, although beaten, the Hittites remained a dangerous and powerful foe for Egypt. In preparation for the inevitable clash with the Hittites, Ramses moved out of Thebes and founded a new city, Pi-Ramses, farther north in Egypt's Nile Delta region; the new location would allow him to quickly respond to any Hittite threat. The city, extending over twelve square miles, had stout walls and may have contained a chariot garrison, parade ground, and workshops.

Recent excavation work at the site of Pi-Ramses has turned up some surprising information. Evidence was found of a huge bronze-smelting works with fifty-foot-long furnaces, which would have been capable of producing several tons of bronze per day. No one had ever imagined that pharaonic Egypt contained such industrial capacity.

The Battle of Kadesh

The confrontation between the two powers came in Ramses' fifth year as pharaoh. He learned that the Hittite king Muwatallis had raised an army of thirty-five thousand men and had equipped the army with several thousand chariots. Worried that the Hittites were massing for an attack on Egyptian territory, Ramses gathered his own forces and set out for Kadesh to meet them, taking a route almost identical to that of Thutmose III nearly two centuries earlier.

The Egyptian army was composed of four infantry divisions named after the gods Amon, Ptah, Seth, and Re, as well as chariots. Crossing the desert in thirty days, the Egyptians camped several miles outside of Kadesh. Some deserters from the Hittite army were brought before the twenty-five-year-old king; they claimed that Muwatallis and his troops had fled before the advancing Egyptian hordes and were actually far to the north.

Eager to take Kadesh, which he believed was held by only a small force, Ramses set out for the city at the head of the Amon division, leaving the rest of his troops to catch up. With his army strung out miles behind him, Ramses reached the outskirts of Kadesh. There, his sentries caught two Hittite spies. After being beaten, the spies revealed the terrible truth to the pharaoh: The "deserters" had actually been sent by Muwatallis to trick Ramses. In reality, the entire Hittite army lay hidden just east of Kadesh. Hopelessly outnumbered, Ramses had blundered into a trap.

"All their princes were with him [Muwatallis], and every one of his foot soldiers and chariotry," an Egyptian scribe later wrote. "They covered the mountains and valleys and were like locusts in their multitude."[45]

As Ramses and his officers frantically made emergency plans, Muwatallis struck. A wave of Hittite chariots plowed into the Egyptian division of Re, which was just coming up to support their pharaoh, and scattered it in all directions. Then the Hittites attacked Ramses. Panicked, many Egyptian soldiers fled.

Ramses, however, was not one of them. Instead of retreating, the pharaoh charged the enemy in his chariot. Fighting like a man

Ramses' reputation as a military genius stems mostly from a battle with the Hittites at Kadesh. Though Ramses claimed victory, most historians consider it a draw.

possessed, Ramses repeatedly attacked the Hittite hordes, trying to break through and reach the remainder of his army. At one point his charioteer, realizing the overwhelming odds facing them, appealed to his king:

> My good lord, valiant prince, great protector of Egypt in the day of battle, we stand alone in the midst of the foe. Behold,

the foot-soldiery and chariotry have abandoned us. Wherefore wilt thou stay until they bereave us of breath? Let us remain unscathed, save us, Ramses![46]

The pharaoh attempted to reassure his soldier:

Steady, steady thine heart, my charioteer. I shall enter in among them even as a hawk striketh; I slay, hew in pieces, and cast to the ground. What mean these cowards to me? My face groweth not pale for a million of them.[47]

True to his word, Ramses did not falter. Although the Egyptians shrouded actual details of the Battle of Kadesh in hyperbole and exaggeration (including the notion that, by himself, Ramses fended off *all* the enemy soldiers), there seems little doubt that the pharaoh's fierce resistance and courage in the face of overwhelming odds rallied his troops, who came storming back to his aid. Some experts also believe that Ramses was aided by other elements of his army coming up at a critical point in the battle and attacking the weary Hittites.

But no matter how he did it, Ramses escaped the Hittite ambush and joined up with the remainder of his army. He then attacked the Hittites, forcing them to fall back into Kadesh.

The next day Ramses counterattacked, but the Hittite forces were too strong. The battle ended with the pharaoh retreating toward Egypt.

Out of everything that he would accomplish during his six decades as pharaoh, the Battle of Kadesh was Ramses' finest hour. He returned to Egypt proclaiming a great victory over the country's bitter foe, and scribes immediately began recording details of his triumph. Not only did the king build monuments, obelisks, and temples on which the story of the battle was portrayed, he also had it placed on the monuments of other pharaohs. An Egyptian citizen could hardly be unaware of Ramses' "magnificent" victory at Kadesh. As Egyptologist John Wilson notes, "There is no episode in Egyptian history that occupies so much carved wall space in Egyptian temples"[48] as the Battle of Kadesh. It was also the subject of the epic poem *Pentaur,* one of the longest texts in Egyptian history.

But while Ramses lost no opportunity to extol his glorious victory, the truth was somewhat different. Although he had indeed fought like a tiger on the first day of the battle and succeeded in rallying the Egyptian army, ultimately Ramses did not force the

Hittites to withdraw. They remained in control of Kadesh and the territory they had taken. While the Hittites had been stopped from encroaching farther into Egyptian territory, they had not been destroyed. They remained a potent and dangerous foe.

Many Egyptian scholars consider the Battle of Kadesh a draw. (In fact, Hittite documents claimed they had won.) As historian Leonard Cottrell writes, "Perhaps the basic truth is that the two great powers, after their trial of strength, realized that neither could overcome the other."[49]

Ramses' reputation as a military genius rests almost solely on Kadesh. Since Ramses himself tells the story of the battle, some Egyptian experts question the portrait that has come down throughout history of the pharaoh as a magnificent warrior. They point out that he was easily duped, almost got his army destroyed, and was nearly killed.

There seems little doubt, however, that Egyptians believed this portrait, thanks to Ramses' relentless recitation of his version of the battle. While Ramses may not have been the greatest warrior, he may have been history's first "spin doctor" (a person who reports the details of an event in such a way as to make it appear favorable).

Ramses Makes Peace

In the tenth year of Ramses' reign, his adversary Muwatallis died. An uneasy calm descended over relations between the Hittites and the Egyptians. Finally, in the twenty-first year of his reign, Ramses and the Hittite king Hattusilis III signed a peace treaty. This is one of the first peace treaties in history for which the text has been preserved so that it can be studied today. In the treaty, both Egypt and the Hittites pledged to come to each other's aid if attacked and to respect each other's borders.

Thirteen years later, with the treaty still in effect, Ramses married a Hittite princess, further reinforcing the bonds between the once-bitter enemies. However, evidence suggests that even though the two sides were no longer at war, they were also not the best of friends. When the princess was late in arriving for the wedding ceremony, Ramses complained to the Hittites that he lacked both the girl and her dowry. The Hittite queen Pudoukhepa retorted: "You shouldn't be suspicious of us, but trust us. . . . It is neither friendly nor honorable . . . that you, my brother, want to become rich at my expense!"[50] (Ramses, perhaps remembering what had happened to Tutankhamon's widow when she tried to marry a foreigner, sent a military escort to bring his Hittite bride to Egypt.)

But all was forgotten when the young woman arrived and dazzled the king with her beauty and charm:

> Now she was beautiful in the opinion of His Majesty, and he loved her more than anything, as a momentous event for him, a triumph. She was installed in the Royal Palace, accompanying the Sovereign daily, her name radiant in the land.[51]

While it might be surprising that two hostile powers such as Egypt and the Hittites would sign a peace treaty, some experts now believe there was another reason that drove Ramses to it: the Exodus of the Jews.

Some Egyptologists speculate that Ramses II is the unnamed pharaoh referred to in the biblical story of the Exodus. According to the account, the pharaoh released the Jews from slavery and allowed them to follow Moses to freedom after the god of the Israelites sent ten plagues against Egypt. The last plague killed the firstborn child of all Egyptians.

Ramses' firstborn son was named Amunherkopshef. His death is placed by Egyptologists around 1262 B.C., which is also when the Exodus is thought to have occurred. (The exact date is unknown, since there is virtually no archaeological evidence to support the Exodus and Egyptian records ignore it.) According to one theory, the death of his firstborn son turned Ramses' thoughts from war to peace, and so he ended his long-running conflict with the Hittites.

The Monument Builder

The Hittite peace treaty freed Ramses from military matters and enabled him to concentrate on the other great achievement of his reign: building. Sparked by his zeal for self-promotion, Ramses was the most prolific builder in ancient Egyptian history. The pharaoh built temples, statues, monuments, and other structures throughout the Nile valley.

One reason that he was able to build so much so soon was that Ramses preferred incised carvings, which could be produced quickly and were difficult to erase by future rulers who wanted to usurp his buildings for their own purposes. Even today, thousands of years after their construction, some of Ramses' buildings still survive, inspiring awe and disbelief at their sheer size and majesty.

The pharaoh seems to have taken a personal interest in the stone used in constructing many of his buildings. In his youth

Ramses had been sent by his father, Seti, to oversee the operations at his granite quarry in Aswan. Thus, the pharaoh considered himself an expert on the types of stone to use; at Aswan, an inscription describes how the king once told his sculptors that he had personally "examined a fine mountain in order that I might give you the use of it."[52] Another time, during a stroll in the desert, Ramses found a large deposit of very rare and extremely durable quartzite. The pharaoh immediately set his sculptors to work on this block; although they supposedly chiseled it into a gigantic statue of Ramses that was later erected in Pi-Ramses, it has never been found.

Of everything built by Ramses, the colossal temple at Abu Simbel is the most famous. Egyptian temples were usually constructed out of blocks of stone fitted together and then carved, but Abu Simbel was carved *into* a sandstone cliff at a depth of nearly two hundred feet. A smaller temple, dedicated by Ramses to his favorite queen, Nefertari, as well as to Hathor, the goddess of love, was also built at Abu Simbel.

The large temple has four gigantic seated statues of Ramses, each approximately sixty-five feet high, guarding the front. (The top portion of one statue collapsed long ago.) Smaller figures of some of the pharaoh's wives and children are beside the legs of the larger statues.

The most famous of Ramses' building exploits is the massive temple at Abu Simbel. The temple is actually carved two hundred feet into the sandstone cliffs.

These are two of the many colossal statues that decorate the temple at Abu Simbel. The temple was situated so that it is bathed in the sunlight of every new morning.

The great temple is precisely situated so that it is bathed in the light of each new day. In the late 1840s, Florence Nightingale journeyed to Egypt and described dawn at Abu Simbel:

> We clambered and slid through the avalanche of sand, which now [at that time] separates the two temples. There they sit, the four mighty colossi. Before sunrise we were watching for the first rays. The day broke; the top of the rock became golden—the golden rays crept down—one colossus gave a radiant smile, as his own glorious sun reached him.[53]

Inside the large temple, which is about 180 feet deep, are numerous halls and chambers leading to a central sanctuary deep within the structure. In this sanctuary is a statue of Ramses II, plus statues of the three gods to whom the temple is dedicated (Amon-Re, Ptah, and Re-Harakhte). Twice each year, on February 22 and October 22, the rays of the rising sun penetrate the temple and strike these four statues.

If Ramses had built only Abu Simbel, the sheer size and the grandeur of the temple are sufficient to make his name live forever. But the king did not stop there.

At Karnak, as part of a temple to Amon, Ramses built the famous Hypostyle Hall (the name comes from a Greek word meaning "to rest on pillars"), whose roof rests on 122 columns that are 70 feet tall. Built in nine rows, the columns are so massive (328 feet from side to side and 164 feet from front to back) that one hundred people could stand atop each. In ancient times the Hypostyle Hall was considered an architectural wonder.

Another famous structure built by Ramses is the mortuary temple complex known as the Ramesseum. Within the large complex were two forecourts, a hypostyle hall, antechambers, a sanctuary, and subsidiary rooms. The Ramesseum contained a sixty-foot tall, one-thousand-ton statue of Ramses, which later toppled over. (Today the head and torso of the statue remain where they fell, but other parts are displayed in museums throughout the world.)

Another of Ramses' many impressive monuments is the mortuary complex known as the Ramesseum. It contained a statue of Ramses that weighed over one thousand tons.

Here, as virtually everywhere else, Ramses inscribed his "victory" at Kadesh.

These are just a few of the many temples, statues, obelisks, and other structures completed during Ramses' reign. Just like the story of the Battle of Kadesh, an Egyptian during Ramses' regime could not escape seeing something built by their king. When he did not build his own structures from the ground up, he appropriated the structures of other pharaohs and put his name on them. He even demolished existing buildings and took the stones and raw materials for his own use. Thousands of years later, when ancient Egypt's civilization was first rediscovered, Ramses' buildings were so numerous, and accounts of his military exploits so plentiful, that early Egyptologists thought he must have been the mightiest pharaoh in history and dubbed him Ramses the Great.

This sarcophagus housed the remains of Ramses' first wife, Nefertari. Although she was just one of his many wives and mistresses—with whom he fathered as many as 100 children—it appears that she was his favorite.

His monuments survived, thousands of years later, displaying the force of his personality across the ages. In the 1830s the French removed an obelisk constructed by Ramses at the Luxor temple, and brought it back to France to commemorate Napoléon's Egyptian expedition during 1798 and 1799. Erected in Paris, the obelisk displayed Ramses' description of his reign as king, its inscription still bold and proud after two thousand years: "A ruler great in wrath, mighty in strength, every land trembles at him, because of his renown."[54]

Ramses the Man

While his buildings remain eternal monuments to the glory of his reign, little is known about Ramses himself. He was very fond of his first queen, Nefertari, who bore him six children. Among her many royal and official titles, such as "Great Royal Wife," are some that indicate the pharaoh's genuine affection for her, such as "Lady of Charm," "Beautiful of Face," and "Sweet of Love." On Nefertari's temple at Abu Simbel Ramses had inscribed "She for whom the sun doth shine."

Unfortunately, by the time Abu Simbel was dedicated in approximately 1266 B.C., Ramses' favorite queen was near the end of her life. No further images of her have been discovered after this time, and it is assumed that she died soon after the ceremonies honoring her and Ramses at Abu Simbel.

Between Nefertari and his numerous wives and mistresses, Ramses fathered about one hundred children, with an equal number of boys and girls. He had reddish blond hair (possibly as a result of dye; his natural color was auburn), a strong jaw, beaked nose, and a long, thin face. At approximately five feet eight inches, Ramses was taller than most Egyptians (who averaged five feet three inches in height).

Although the first years of Ramses' reign were filled with important events, little of significance seems to have occurred after the Hittite peace treaty. Some experts believe this is because the king focused primarily on his numerous building projects and delegated the daily details of running the country to his administrators. As biographer Olivier Tiano writes,

> The absence of important events after the treaty with the Hittites, the activities of some other princes, and the power of a small number of high dignitaries suggest that the king— burdened by the prestige of his exploits— progressively delegates the essential duties of his authority, remaining primarily concerned with his own deification for almost two-thirds of his long reign.[55]

Ramses II died at around age ninety, which was extraordinarily old by Egyptian standards. (Most Egyptians only lived until their mid-thirties.) His sixty-seven-year reign was the second longest in Egypt's history, eclipsed only by Pharaoh Pepi II of the Sixth Dynasty, who ruled for about ninety years. For many Egyptians, Ramses was the only pharaoh they ever knew.

Ramses ruled Egypt for more than six decades and died at what was then the very old age of ninety.

At his death Ramses suffered from numerous illnesses. An examination of his mummy revealed that he probably had ankylosis spondylitis, a disease in which the bones of the spinal column gradually fuse together. His back was so badly bent when he died that the embalmers had to break his spine to keep his head up. He also had problems with his hips, and a blood circulation condition that further limited his mobility in later years. He also suffered from abscesses in his jaw.

The reign of Ramses II was the last great era for ancient Egypt. After his death the country began a long, slow decline. New threats from abroad stripped Egypt of its empire, taking away the source of the wealth that had sustained the country and triggering an economic crisis. The power of the priests continued to grow and a succession of weak and ineffective pharaohs reduced the monarchy to second-rate status. While other pharaohs took the name Ramses to forge a link, however puny, with their illustrious predecessor, only Ramses III demonstrated the courage and wisdom to arrest the general decline of the Egyptian state.

There was only one Ramses the Great.

Ramses Rediscovered

Although Ramses II lived thousands of years ago, he continues to influence the modern world.

The magnificent temples at Abu Simbel were unknown to the Western world until 1813, when they were discovered by Swiss explorer Johann Ludwig Burckhardt as he came over a mountain and saw the facade of the larger temple. The fame of these temples quickly grew; by the Victorian era, they were the favorite attraction of English tourists, even though they were often deeply obscured by sand.

After surviving every natural assault for thousands of years, the temples at Abu Simbel faced their biggest crisis in 1964. Construction of the Aswan Dam was causing water levels to rise in Lake Nasser (the lake was the dam's reservoir); eventually the waters would cover the temples. With the support of the United Nations Educational, Scientific and Cultural Organization (UNESCO), the Egyptian government issued a worldwide appeal for help in saving the legendary structures.

A team of international experts raced to the scene and decided to cut apart the temples and reconstruct them on the same cliff two hundred feet higher. Over the next four years the temples were cut into over one thousand blocks, some of them weighing as much as thirty tons, and were painstakingly rebuilt in the same position to each other as well as to the rising sun as they had been by the ancient Egyptians. The operation received worldwide attention; centuries after his death, the name of Ramses was once again the topic of conversation throughout the world.

A few years after this, Ramses II once again dominated the headlines. In 1977 his mummy, which had been found in 1881 along with numerous other royal mummies that had been sent to Cairo (where they were labeled as "dried fish" by customs officials who had no classification for mummies) to be put on display, was flown to Paris to receive treatment for an infection that was destroying it. Upon its arrival at the Paris airport, the mummy of Ramses was accorded the same honors, amid great fanfare, as any visiting head of state. Once the infection was cured, Ramses' mummy was returned to Cairo.

Even in the 1990s, Ramses continued to make news. In 1995, American archaeologist Kent Weeks discovered a sprawling tomb built by the pharaoh in the Valley of the Kings. The find is considered the most significant in Egypt since the discovery of Tutankhamon's tomb. By October 1997 over 108 rooms had been uncovered, with more expected as excavations continued. At that point, inscriptions for Ramses II and at least four of his sons had been found in the mausoleum.

No one knows why Ramses built the tomb, how many of his children are buried there, or why there are so many rooms. The only certainty is that in death, as in life, Ramses the Great continues to dominate all things Egyptian.

CHAPTER 6

Cleopatra: The End of Egyptian Independence

Although she was reputed to be beautiful, it was via her wits that Cleopatra ruled Egypt. But her Egypt was a thousand years removed from the country that had been the master of the ancient world. Betrayed by a long succession of weak kings and battered by a series of invasions and conquests by foreign powers, Cleopatra's Egypt was like a wounded animal—its pulse was faint and its vital signs were weak. Cleopatra dreamed of restoring Egypt's health by bringing back the days of pharaonic glory. Ultimately, however, she hastened its demise.

Cleopatra's Rise to Power

After the death of Alexander the Great in 323 B.C., his vast empire was divided among his generals. Egypt was taken by Ptolemy Soter, who wanted to rule in the grand pharaonic tradition. Ptolemy declared himself king of Egypt in 304 B.C., thus beginning the Ptolemaic dynasty that governed the country for the next 250 years. To strengthen his association with Egypt's past, Ptolemy claimed to be a living god, just like the pharaohs. He also revived the tradition of brother/sister marriages in the royal family.

Although the Ptolemaic kings tried to respect Egyptian culture, the country took on a distinctive Greek flavor. The official language of the Egyptian government was Greek; only priests used hieroglyphs. The Ptolemies used Egypt's bountiful agricultural harvests to rebuild the economy and make the country an important trading partner with other lands. However, it was primarily upper-class Greek citizens who benefited from the economic prosperity; the Egyptian peasants who toiled in the fields and made up the overwhelming majority of the country's population received almost nothing. Gradually Egyptians became second-class citizens in their own land.

Cleopatra VII was born in 69 B.C., the third of six children of King Ptolemy XII. Although the identity of her mother is unknown, some have identified her as Cleopatra V Tryphaeana, who was both wife and sister of Ptolemy XII.

According to legend, Cleopatra was a ravishing beauty whom men found irresistible. Unfortunately, no contemporary description of her exists, so her appearance is open to speculation. The Greek biographer Plutarch, writing two hundred years after her death, claimed that Cleopatra was not beautiful at all. Instead, he credited her with a musical voice, great charm, and a forceful character. Since her ancestors were probably of Middle Eastern origin, it is likely that Cleopatra's complexion was dark.

The Ptolemaic dynasty, of which Cleopatra (pictured) was a part, was descended from Ptolemy Soter, one of Alexander the Great's generals.

Although she eventually became queen of Egypt, Cleopatra probably did not consider herself an Egyptian. The language, culture, and education of the Ptolemies was Greek, and Cleopatra almost certainly would have considered herself Greek as well.

By the time of Cleopatra's birth, Rome had swallowed much of the Ptolemies' former empire. It was only through a policy of alliance and friendship with the powerful Romans that the Ptolemies remained on the Egyptian throne. In 57 B.C., unrest in Egypt temporarily deposed Ptolemy XII; he was restored to the Egyptian throne with the help of a Roman military force, including a young cavalry officer named Mark Antony.

Over the years the Ptolemaic custom of brother/sister royal marriages resulted in numerous royal intrigues as family members fought and even murdered each other to rule Egypt. When Ptolemy XII was temporarily overthrown in 57, his place was initially taken by his daughter Cleopatra VI. She, in turn, was either killed or deposed by her sister and another of Ptolemy's daughters, Berenice IV. When Ptolemy was restored to the throne, he executed Berenice.

Berenice's death made Cleopatra VII next in line to inherit the Egyptian throne. However, in Ptolemaic Egypt a queen could not rule without a king. Thus, when Ptolemy XII died in 51, his will named both eighteen-year-old Cleopatra and ten-year-old Ptolemy XIII as joint heirs. This meant that both would now succeed to the throne.

Although she was Greek in upbringing, Cleopatra seems to have had good relations with the native Egyptian population. Plutarch said that she spoke Egyptian—the only one of the Ptolemies to ever do so. She also participated in some Egyptian religious ceremonies.

But this goodwill did not help Cleopatra when she arrested the men responsible for the murder of the two sons of the pro-Roman governor of Syria who had come to beg Cleopatra to send troops to help remove some Parthians from their country. This caused the relationship between Cleopatra and her brother and coregent, Ptolemy XIII, to unravel. Aiding the powerful Romans was not popular with young Ptolemy's Greek-oriented advisers. As her brother began to assert himself more and more, Cleopatra was forced into the background. Finally, sometime between June and September of 49, Cleopatra was forced off the throne of Egypt, leaving her younger brother as sole ruler.

Cleopatra needed Roman help to hold on to her claim to the throne of Egypt. Julius Caesar (pictured) came to her aid and the two eventually became lovers.

Julius Caesar

At this time in Rome, a civil war was raging between generals Julius Caesar and Pompey the Great. After being defeated at Pharsalus in central Greece in 48, Pompey fled to Egypt, where he hoped to raise a new army and continue the struggle against Caesar. In September 48, however Pompey was murdered by the Egyptians, who had no desire to antagonize the victor of Pharsalus. When Caesar arrived in Egypt in pursuit of Pompey, he was shown his body. But instead of leaving, as the Egyptians hoped, Caesar announced he would stay until he collected an old debt owed him by the Egyptian government.

Some historians feel that Cleopatra's legendary beauty may have been exaggerated. They believe that she seduced Caesar with her charm and forceful character.

In reality, Caesar needed money to continue paying his troops, and Egypt's wealth was formidable. As the poet Lucan wrote, "He saw the Egyptian wealth with greedy eyes, / And wished some fair pretence to seize the prize."[56]

Caesar knew of the dispute between Cleopatra and Ptolemy XIII, and he felt it was his duty to see that their father's will, which called for them to be joint rulers, should be carried out. Settling into the royal palace in Alexandria, Caesar summoned both Cleopatra and Ptolemy XIII. Ptolemy arrived soon, but Cleopatra, having been removed from the throne and possibly targeted for death by her brother, had more difficulty entering the palace. Somehow, she made the trip without being seen by Ptolemy's agents. (The legend says she hid herself in a roll of carpet or bedding that was carried into the palace by a merchant named Apollodorus, who then unrolled it in front of Caesar, who was stunned to see Cleopatra tumble out.)

Cleopatra captivated the worldly (and already married) Roman general, and the two became lovers. Historian Michael Grant explains why the fifty-two-year-old Caesar, an experienced lover, would have been attracted to the twenty-one-year-old Cleopatra: Not only was she intelligent and quick-witted, but Cleopatra was also descended from Ptolemy I, a relative of Alexander the Great; in addition, as queen of Egypt, Cleopatra was a descendant of all the great pharaohs in her country's long history. It would have been hard for a man with such an acute sense of history as Caesar to turn down a woman with such glamorous ancestors.

As for Cleopatra, the force of Caesar's fame and personality was a great attraction, but he also represented the Roman power that could keep her on the throne — a lesson she had learned from her father.

One of the most famous legends of history is that Cleopatra used her great beauty to charm Caesar. Although she was not as breathtaking as commonly believed (coins minted during her reign show her with a hooked nose, prominent chin, and bony face), she was probably attractive. She wore her hair in three distinctive waves, ending with a substantial chignon low on her nape and a few curls hanging both in front of and behind her ears. Like most Egyptian women, she was skilled at using cosmetics to accent her appearance.

The artistic representations of Cleopatra suggest that her physical beauty was somewhat overstated by writers and historians. Often portrayed with a hooked nose and bony face, she had an irresistible presence nonetheless.

According to Plutarch, however, Cleopatra had other attributes besides her appearance:

Her own beauty, so we are told, was not of that incomparable kind which instantly captivates the beholder. But the charm of her presence was irresistible, and there was an attraction in her person and her talk, together with a peculiar force of character which pervaded her every word and action, and laid all who associated with her under its spell.[57]

When Ptolemy XIII saw that his rival and Caesar were lovers, he cried out to his supporters that he had been betrayed. Caesar ruled that both Ptolemy and Cleopatra should rule Egypt together, as their father's will had stipulated, but this compromise lasted only a few months. War ultimately broke out between the two sides. Caesar, fighting on behalf of the now-pregnant Cleopatra, defeated Ptolemy in battle in March 47. Weighed down by his golden armor, the fifteen-year-old king drowned in the Nile while trying to flee with his defeated army. Although, in keeping with Ptolemaic tradition, Caesar appointed Cleopatra's other half brother, twelve-year-old Ptolemy XIV, as her coregent, in essence Cleopatra was now the sole ruler of Egypt.

Cleopatra Goes to Rome

Caesar returned to Rome in the summer of 47 B.C.. Soon after giving birth, Cleopatra also came to Rome. She named the infant boy Ptolemy Caesar; others called him Caesarion. Both titles were meant to indicate that the child was Caesar's, but he never publicly acknowledged this.

One possible reason for Cleopatra's trip to Rome was to continue her affair with Caesar. If that was so, she had plenty of company. Besides his wife, Calpurnia, Caesar also supposedly had mistresses. Caesar obligingly housed Cleopatra at his own estate, but given the pressure of Caesar's position, it is unlikely that the two shared much time together.

Cleopatra remained in Rome until Julius Caesar was assassinated on March 15, 44 B.C.. In his will, Caesar made no mention of either Cleopatra or Caesarion. Instead, it stipulated that his nineteen-year-old grand-nephew Gaius Octavius (soon to become known as Octavian), should become his adopted son after his death. Realizing that the lives of both herself and Caesarion were now in great danger, Cleopatra and her son returned to Egypt. Soon after her arrival, her half brother and coregent, Ptolemy XIV, died. Moving quickly, Cleopatra named her three-year-old son as her joint ruler. The convenience of Ptolemy XIV's death has led many researchers to charge that Cleopatra murdered him.

Cleopatra ran Egypt for the next few years. In both 42 and 41 B.C., the Nile failed to rise enough to adequately flood the land, and Egypt's agricultural production suffered. Not only did this hamper the country's ability to sell crops and make money, but it also caused famine throughout Egypt.

In spite of these difficulties, Cleopatra assembled a fleet of Egyptian ships and troops and sailed to join Mark Antony and

Octavian. The two were leading the pro-Caesar forces against the anti-Caesar forces in the Roman civil war, which had broken out after Caesar's murder. Ill health, and a storm that shattered the Egyptian fleet off the coast of Africa, forced Cleopatra to return to Alexandria.

Mark Antony

Cleopatra, though, could not escape events in Rome. The pro-Caesar forces were victorious in the civil war. This led to three men (called a triumvirate) running the Roman Empire: Octavian, Lepidus, and Mark Antony. Trying to consolidate his position, Antony decided to lead a military campaign against Rome's most formidable enemy, the Parthian Empire (modern-day Iran and Afghanistan). Seeking money and materials for the venture, Antony went to Egypt to see Cleopatra.

There are several similarities between Julius Caesar and Mark Antony and their visits to Egypt: Both sought money for military expeditions; both were married; and both were captivated by Cleopatra.

Antony summoned Cleopatra to the ancient city of Tarsus. Obviously trying to make a good impression on the man who might well succeed Julius Caesar, Cleopatra spared no expense. Her arrival at Tarsus was described by Plutarch:

Cleopatra's charms captivated another powerful Roman leader, Mark Antony. Though he was married, Antony eventually fathered three children by Cleopatra.

She came sailing up the river Cydnus in a barge with a poop [stern] of gold, its purple sails billowing in the wind, while her rowers caressed the water with oars of silver which dipped in time to the music of the flute, accompanied by pipes and lutes. Cleopatra herself reclined beneath a canopy of cloth of gold, dressed in the character of Aphrodite (Venus), as we see in her paintings, while on either side to complete the picture stood boys costumed as Cupids who cooled her with their fans.[58]

As with Caesar, Cleopatra enamored Antony and the two became lovers. The relationship between Antony and Cleopatra is one of history's most famous love stories. Ultimately, she bore him three children. Yet underneath their personal relationship was hardheaded reality: Antony needed Cleopatra's money, and she needed his political and military support.

In return for her monetary and military aid in his quest against Octavian to succeed Julius Caesar, Mark Antony (pictured) gave Cleopatra sizable territories in the Middle East.

Cleopatra agreed to finance Antony's Parthian campaign in exchange for his support against her enemies. On her instructions, Antony had several people killed whom Cleopatra considered rivals, including her half sister Arsinoe and a youth who claimed to be her half brother and former rival, Ptolemy XIII, whom everyone believed had drowned.

Antony spent the winter of 41–40 B.C. with Cleopatra. During this time she again became pregnant, and there was little doubt that Antony was the father. However, problems both in Rome and abroad forced Antony to postpone his Parthian campaign. He left Cleopatra in the early months of 40; he would not see her again for nearly four years.

During these years Cleopatra again concentrated on running the country and, by most accounts, she did a good job. She enriched Egypt's coffers by negotiating profitable deals for oil, dates, and balsam with other rulers. She also, in the autumn of 40, gave birth to Antony's twins, whom she named Alexander and Cleopatra. It is unknown whether she and Antony wrote to each other during their long separation. However, Cleopatra did keep informed about his whereabouts through an Egyptian astrologer who traveled with Antony.

In the autumn of 37 B.C. Antony returned to Egypt, ready to resume his Parthian campaign and again seeking money and supplies from Cleopatra. In return for her support, Cleopatra received from him Roman territories in what is today Lebanon, Syria, Jordan, and southern Turkey. Without fighting a single battle, Cleopatra had taken a giant step toward restoring the once-mighty Egyptian Empire.

Antony spent the winter of 37–36 with Cleopatra. By the time he was ready to embark on his Parthian campaign in mid-May 36, the Egyptian queen was again pregnant with his child. Both Cleopatra and Antony expected that he would win a glorious victory against the Parthians and secure himself as Caesar's successor. Unfortunately, it was not to be. His Parthian campaign was a disaster. By the time he returned to safety in Syria, he had lost two-fifths of his troops. To make matters worse, at almost the same time (September 36 B.C.), Antony's bitter rival Octavian had defeated a group of pirates that was threatening Roman security, thus establishing himself as a superb military leader and elevating his stature as Caesar's possible successor.

Almost immediately upon his return to Syria, Antony sent for Cleopatra. Although this summons is often portrayed as a lovesick plea by Antony to his lover, in reality he needed the supplies and money that Cleopatra could bring to his battered troops. Cleopatra had just given birth to her fourth child (her third by Antony), Ptolemy Philadelphus. Nevertheless, she gathered all the aid she could and arrived in Syria in January.

Meanwhile, in Rome, Octavian was busily spreading stories about how Cleopatra had

By helping Antony, Cleopatra hoped to restore the glory of pharaonic Egypt.

used her sexual wiles to ensnare Antony and befuddle his mind. As the rivalry increased between Antony and Octavian, the drumbeat of accusations against Cleopatra grew louder; by the time of their final showdown, most Romans probably considered her to be the most evil temptress of all time. The success of Octavian's propaganda campaign has echoed across the centuries; today, the popular image of Cleopatra as a woman whose beauty clouded men's minds is a direct result of the seeds Octavian planted.

Unfortunately, Antony picked this moment to lend credibility to Octavian's charges. In the spring of 35, Octavia, sister of Octavian and Antony's wife, also gathered supplies for Antony's army and was personally bringing them to him in Syria, where he was with Cleopatra. Antony sent a letter to his wife in Athens, requesting that the supplies be sent to him but asking her to return to Rome. This snub rallied Roman public opinion to Octavia's side, and against Antony and Cleopatra.

The Donations of Alexandria

Then, in the autumn of 34 B.C., after a minor military victory, Antony staged an opulent ceremony known as the Donations of Alexandria. Sitting on a golden throne on a platform of silver and dressed like the god Dionysus, Antony gave Cleopatra's four children vast amounts of land belonging to the Roman Empire, as well as some kingdoms and territories that had not even been conquered yet. He also declared Cleopatra "Queen of Kings" and Caesarion "King of Kings." He said that Caesarion was the only real son of Julius Caesar and thus, his only true heir—a claim that angered Octavian. Cleopatra, who also presided over the ceremony on a golden throne, was dressed like the goddess Isis.

To worried Romans, it seemed as if Antony was setting up Caesarion to rule over Rome and the western part of their empire, and Cleopatra (through her children) to govern an expanded Ptolemaic empire in the east. For years Romans had worried over prophecies that a mighty empire would arise in the east and end Rome's world domination. To many citizens, it seemed as if the Donations of Alexandria was setting the stage for these prophecies to come true.

As for Cleopatra, her dream of returning Egypt to its former glory seemed about to be fulfilled. To celebrate the Donations of Alexandria, she had a special coin imprinted with her portrait; on it her face is sterner, her hook nose is even more pronounced, and her hair is worn in a cluster of curls around her face, which descend to a small knot at the nape of her neck.

Cleopatra often worn pearls in her hair, which were extremely expensive at this time. According to a famous story, to impress Antony with her wealth, Cleopatra supposedly dropped a pearl into a cup of vinegar, waited until it dissolved, and then drank it. (Since vinegar does not dissolve pearls, however, this story is obviously false.)

War

Inevitably, the widening gulf between Antony and Octavian led to war between them. Antony and Cleopatra's forces gathered at Actium on the southern shore of the Gulf of Ambracia off the Greek coast. Moving swiftly, Octavian's ships blocked the entrance to

On September 2, 31 B.C., Mark Antony and Cleopatra's fleet engaged the forces of Octavian at Actium. Antony and Cleopatra were badly defeated, and Octavian eventually became Augustus, the first Roman emperor.

the gulf, trapping Cleopatra's fleet, and his army threatened Actium from the north. Antony was more skilled at fighting on land, but to do so would mean abandoning Cleopatra's fleet. The queen successfully argued for a sea battle. Although legend says that Antony agreed with Cleopatra because he was blinded by love, in reality he could do little else. He needed Cleopatra and her fleet.

The Battle of Actium, fought on September 2, 31 B.C., was a disaster for Antony and Cleopatra. According to Plutarch, once an escape route became available, Cleopatra sailed away with her fleet early in the fight, and Antony followed her in another ship. Demoralized, the remainder of Antony's forces both on land and sea surrendered to Octavian.

It is uncertain why Cleopatra fled when she did or why Antony abandoned his troops to join her. One possible explanation is that it had all been prearranged; hemmed in by Octavian, Antony and Cleopatra might have agreed to escape at the earliest opportunity to regroup their forces and to live to fight another day. Upon her return to Egypt, Cleopatra is supposed to have acted as if she and Antony had won a great victory.

In reality, however, the defeat at Actium spelled the end of Cleopatra's dream to return Egypt to its former glory. Most of Cleopatra's and Antony's allies switched allegiance to Octavian, and it was just a matter of time until he took Alexandria and Egypt itself. During the months that followed Actium, as Cleopatra frantically tried to formulate strategy, Antony was paralyzed by depression and self-pity.

On August 1, 30, Octavian took Alexandria as the remnants of Antony's army offered token resistance. Believing all was lost and that Cleopatra was dead, Antony tried to kill himself by plunging a sword into his body. However, the blow was not immediately fatal. As he lay dying, word came to him that Cleopatra was still alive and had taken refuge in her mausoleum. The bleeding Antony was carried to her but, because the building had been barricaded, he had to be hoisted in through an upstairs window. As Plutarch writes,

> Those who were present say that there was never a more pitiable sight than the spectacle of Antony, covered with blood, struggling in his death agonies and stretching out his hands towards Cleopatra as he swung helplessly in the air. The task [of pulling him through the window] was almost beyond a woman's strength, and it was only with great difficulty that Cleopatra, clinging with both hands to the rope

and with the muscles of her face distorted by the strain, was able to haul him up, while those on the ground encouraged her with their cries and shared her agony.[59]

Antony died soon after, and Cleopatra was taken prisoner by Octavian. Worried that he was going to bring her to Rome and parade her through the streets in chains, as had been done to other defeated foes, Cleopatra planned to commit suicide.

The Death of Cleopatra

A furious historical debate surrounds the manner of Cleopatra's death on August 12, 30 B.C. The most common belief is that she died from the bite of a poisonous snake, which was smuggled in to her, but this is uncertain. The only marks found on her body were two small scratches on her arm. Even Plutarch, who read the writings of Cleopatra's personal physician, was not sure how she died. Other theories are that she used poison hidden in a hairpin or comb.

The snake that is often thought to have caused her death is an asp, a term commonly applied to various varieties of the north African viper. However, biographer Lucy Hughes-Hallet notes that death from a viper bite is not only extremely unpleasant and painful but also causes vomiting and loss of bodily functions—certainly not the dignified death that Cleopatra would have sought. Instead, Hughes-Hallet speculates that a cobra, whose bite causes a paralysis much like sleep, was the likely vehicle that ended the queen's life.

When several of Octavian's troops burst into Cleopatra's quarters, they found her already dead. One of her maids was also dead, and a second maid, near death, was struggling to adjust the crown on her queen's head.

"Charmion," cried a guard to the maid, "was this right?"

"It is entirely right," gasped the maid, "and fitting for a queen descended from so many kings."[60]

Cleopatra's death spelled the end of Egypt as an independent nation. Octavian, who in the year 27 B.C. took the name Augustus Caesar and became the first Roman emperor, made Egypt into just another province of the Roman Empire. Cleopatra's dreams of restoring the once-mighty Egyptian Empire had failed.

NOTES

Chapter 1: Ancient Egypt

1. Quoted in Jacquetta Hawkes, *Pharaohs of Egypt*. New York: Horizon Caravel Books, 1965.
2. Quoted in Margaret Oliphant, *The Egyptian World*. New York: Warwick Press, 1989.
3. Quoted in Hawkes, *Pharaohs of Egypt*.
4. Quoted in James Putnam, *Eyewitness Books: Mummy*. New York: Knopf, 1993.
5. Quoted in Elizabeth Payne, *The Pharaohs of Ancient Egypt*. New York: Landmark Books, 1964.
6. Quoted in Lionel Casson and the editors of Time-Life Books, *Ancient Egypt*. Alexandria, VA: Time-Life Books, 1965.
7. Quoted in Oliphant, *The Egyptian World*.

Chapter 2: "His Majesty, Herself": Queen Hatshepsut

8. Quoted in Payne, *The Pharaohs of Ancient Egypt*.
9. Quoted in Leonard Cottrell, *The Warrior Pharaohs*. New York: G. P. Putnam's Sons, 1969.
10. Quoted in Cottrell, *The Warrior Pharaohs*.
11. Peter A. Clayton, *Chronicle of the Pharaohs*. London: Thames and Hudson, 1994.
12. Joyce Tyldesley, *Hatchepsut: The Female Pharaoh*. New York: Penguin Books, 1998.
13. Tyldesley, *Hatchepsut*.
14. Payne, *The Pharaohs of Ancient Egypt*.
15. Evelyn Wells, *Hatshepsut*. Garden City, NY: Doubleday, 1969.
16. Tyldesley, *Hatchepsut*.
17. Quoted from *The Story of Hatshepsut*, http://www.duke.edu/~drb3/hatshepsut/hatshepsut.html.
18. Quoted in Paul Johnson, *The Civilization of Ancient Egypt*. New York: Atheneum, 1978.
19. Quoted in Payne, *The Pharaohs of Ancient Egypt*.
20. Quoted in Cottrell, *The Warrior Pharaohs*.
21. Nicolas Grimal, *A History of Ancient Egypt*. Oxford: Blackwell, 1992.
22. Tyldesley, *Hatchepsut*.
23. Quoted in Tyldesley, *Hatchepsut*.
24. Quoted in Tyldesley, *Hatchepsut*.
25. Tyldesley, *Hatchepsut*.
26. Quoted in Wells, *Hatshepsut*.
27. Quoted in Tyldesley, *Hatchepsut*.

Chapter 3: Akhenaten: Heretic or Visionary?

28. Quoted in Editors of Time-Life Books, *Egypt: Land of the Pharaohs*. Alexandria, VA: Time-Life Books, 1992.
29. Quoted from *Neferneferuaten-Nefertiti*, available from

http://www.malone.org/~jrodrigu/isis/queen.html.
30. Quoted in Cyril Aldred, *Akhenaten: King of Egypt*. London: Thames and Hudson, 1988.
31. Peter A. Clayton, *Chronicle of the Pharaohs*. London: Thames and Hudson, 1994.
32. "The Amarna Revolution," available from www.stetson.edu~psteeves/classes/aten.html.
33. Quoted in Editors, *Egypt*.
34. Quoted in Payne, *The Pharaohs of Ancient Egypt*.
35. Quoted in Editors, *Egypt*.
36. Quoted in Editors, *Egypt*.

Chapter 4: Tutankhamon: Egypt's Most Famous Pharaoh

37. Quoted in Donald B. Redford, *Akhenaten: The Heretic King*. Princeton, NJ: Princeton University Press, 1984.
38. Quoted in Philipp Vandenberg, *The Curse of the Pharaohs*. Philadelphia: J. B. Lippincott, 1975.
39. Quoted in Christiane Desroches-Noblecourt, *Tutankhamen*. Boston: New York Graphic Society, 1976.
40. Quoted in Cottrell, *The Warrior Pharaohs*.
41. Quoted in Vandenberg, *The Curse of the Pharaohs*.
42. Quoted in Vandenberg, *The Curse of the Pharaohs*.
43. Quoted in Vandenberg, *The Curse of the Pharaohs*.

Chapter 5: Ramses II: Egypt's Greatest Pharaoh?

44. Quoted in Editors of Time-Life Books, *Ramses II: Magnificence on the Nile*. Alexandria, VA: Time-Life Books, 1993.
45. Quoted in Cottrell, *The Warrior Pharaohs*.
46. Quoted in Cottrell, *The Warrior Pharaohs*.
47. Quoted in Cottrell, *The Warrior Pharaohs*.
48. Quoted in Payne, *The Pharaohs of Ancient Egypt*.
49. Cottrell, *The Warrior Pharaohs*.
50. Olivier Tiano, *Ramses II and Egypt*. New York: Henry Holt, 1996.
51. Quoted in Editors, *Ramses II*.
52. Quoted in Editors, *Ramses II*.
53. Quoted in Editors, *Egypt*.
54. Quoted in Editors, *Ramses II*.
55. Quoted in Tiano, *Ramses II and Egypt*.

Chapter 6: Cleopatra: The End of Egyptian Independence

56. Quoted in Michael Grant, *Cleopatra*. New York: Simon & Schuster, 1972.
57. Quoted in Grant, *Cleopatra*.
58. Quoted in Grant, *Cleopatra*.
59. Quoted in Lucy Hughes-Hallet, *Cleopatra: Histories, Dreams, and Distortions*. New York: Harper & Row, 1990.
60. Quoted in Grant, *Cleopatra*.

87

For Further Reading

Wendy Boase, *Ancient Egypt*. New York: Gloucester Press, 1978. A good source of general information about ancient Egypt.

Leonard Cottrell, *The Warrior Pharaohs*. New York: G. P. Putnam's Sons, 1969. Although nearly thirty years old, this book is still an informative and accurate source of information on the "fighting" pharaohs.

Geraldine Harris, *Cultural Atlas for Young People: Ancient Egypt*. New York: Facts On File, 1990. Another good source that provides a basic overview of ancient Egypt and the lives of its people. It also contains an easy-to-follow guide to the various dynasties and which pharaohs belonged to each.

George Hart, *Ancient Egypt*. New York: Gulliver Books, 1988. Another good general source of information on Egypt.

Margaret Oliphant, *The Egyptian World*. New York: Warwick Press, 1989. Provides an excellent overview of numerous aspects of Egyptian life.

Mildred Mastin Pace, *Pyramids: Tombs for Eternity*. New York: McGraw-Hill, 1981. A good reference source of how the pyramids were built.

James Putnam, *Eyewitness Books: Mummy*. New York: Knopf, 1993. Along with pyramids, mummies are perhaps the best-known symbol of Egypt. This book discusses not only Egyptian mummies but also those from other societies.

Carter Smith III, *The Pyramid Builders*. Englewood Cliffs, NJ: Silver Burdett Press, 1991. An excellent source of information on that most Egyptian of structures.

Diane Stanley, *Cleopatra*. New York: Morrow Junior Books, 1994. Gives a succinct overview of the entire Cleopatra story from the classical perspective.

Olivier Tiano, *Ramses II and Egypt*. New York: Henry Holt, 1996. Although presented like a children's book, this volume is cleverly written, interesting, and highly informative.

WORKS CONSULTED

Books

Cyril Aldred, *Akhenaten: King of Egypt*. London: Thames and Hudson, 1988. An exceptionally comprehensive examination of the so-called heretic pharaoh.

Lionel Casson, *The Pharaohs*. Chicago: Stonehenge Press, 1981. A good source of general information on the pharaohs and their reigns.

Lionel Casson and the Editors of Time-Life Books, *Ancient Egypt*. Alexandria, VA: Time-Life Books, 1965. An excellent reference book for background and details on ancient Egypt.

Peter A. Clayton, *Chronicle of the Pharaohs*. London: Thames and Hudson, 1994. Contains a large amount of information about each pharaoh in an easy-to-read manner, as well as over three hundred illustrations.

Christiane Desroches-Noblecourt, *Tutankhamen*. Boston: New York Graphic Society, 1976. A book detailing the boy-king's life; it goes into specific detail on the treasures found within his tomb.

Editors of Time-Life Books, *Egypt: Land of the Pharaohs*. Alexandria, VA: Time-Life Books, 1992. Presents information on most of the pharaohs, along with special sections highlighting the discovery of Tutankhamon and other topics.

Editors of Time-Life Books, *Ramses II: Magnificence on the Nile*. Alexandria, VA: Time-Life Books, 1993. One of the best and most up-to-date sources of information on Egypt's master builder, warrior, statesman and public relations genius.

Michael Grant, *Cleopatra*. New York: Simon & Schuster, 1972. A comprehensive biography of Cleopatra, her times, and the two men who meant the most in her life, Mark Antony and Julius Caesar.

Nicolas Grimal, *A History of Ancient Egypt*. Oxford: Blackwell, 1992. Comprehensive study of Egypt and its pharaohs, written in a scholarly manner.

Jacquetta Hawkes, *Pharaohs of Egypt*. New York: Horizon Caravel Books, 1965. Although some of the information is outdated, this book provides a good overview of many of the pharaohs and Egyptian society.

Lucy Hughes-Hallet, *Cleopatra: Histories, Dreams and Distortions*. New York: Harper & Row, 1990. A unique look at the woman and her place in history through a variety of different aspects, including examinations of the "real story," the legends, and the media portrayals.

Paul Johnson, *The Civilization of Ancient Egypt*. New York: Atheneum, 1978. An overall look at the civilization of ancient Egypt and what life was like for the people of this time.

Jaromir Malek, *In the Shadow of the Pyramids*. Norman: University of Oklahoma Press, 1986. A detailed examination of Egypt and the pyramids.

Pierre Montet, *Lives of the Pharaohs*. Cleveland: World, 1968. Although the material is somewhat dated, this book still provides a wealth of information on all the pharaohs, including some of the hard-to-find ones.

Elizabeth Payne, *The Pharaohs of Ancient Egypt*. New York: Landmark Books, 1964. Discusses several of the most well known pharaohs, including Ramses and Tutankhamon.

Donald B. Redford, *Akhenaten: The Heretic King*. Princeton, NJ: Princeton University Press, 1984. A highly readable volume that explores the reign of this most unusual pharaoh.

Henri Stierlin, *The World of the Pharaohs*. New York: Sunflower Books, 1978. Besides providing information about the pharaohs, this book also goes into great depth on the architectural aspects of many of the pharaohs' buildings and temples.

Joyce Tyldesley, *Hatchepsut: The Female Pharaoh*. New York: Penguin Books, 1998. Probably the most comprehensive and up-to-date biography of one of ancient Egypt's most intriguing pharaohs.

Philipp Vandenberg, *The Curse of the Pharaohs*. Philadelphia: J. B. Lippincott, 1975. While examining the so-called curse of Tutankhamon, this book also contains an excellent description of the finding of Tut's tomb.

Evelyn Wells, *Hatshepsut*. Garden City, NY: Doubleday, 1969. A book that attempts to get inside Hatshepsut's head and imagine what her thoughts must have been throughout her extraordinary life.

On-line Sources

Abu Simbel. Available interoz.com/egypt/abusimbel.htm. A page dedicated to the temples at Abu Simbel, complete with an illustration.

The Amarna Revolution. Available www.stetson.edu/~psteeves/classes/aten.html. Text-only summary of the Amarna period during Ankenhaten's reign. Contains the complete text of *Hymn to the Aten*.

The Great Temple of Abu Simbel. Available www.ccer.ggl.ruuni/abu_simbel/abut_simbel.html. A site dedicated to the magnificent temple at Abu Simbel; clicking on the entrance to the temple in the illustration will take you inside the great temple.

The Mysteries of Akhenaten. Available wkweb4.cableinet.co.uk/iwhawkins/egypt.akhmyst.htm. A site discussing Akhenaten, and offering possible reasons for his actions.

Neferneferuaten-Nefertiti. Available www.malone.org/~jrodrigu/isis/queen.html. Contains a brief biography of Nefertiti, along with an illustration.

The Ramesseum. Available www.kv5.com/html/data_ramesseum.html. Provides a brief background of the Ramesseum, along with a diagram of what is contained inside the structure.

The Reign of Akhenaten. Available wkweb4.cableinet.co.uk/iwhawkins/egypt/akhtable.htm. Provides a brief overview of Akhenaten's reign, along with a diagram showing key dates and events.

The Story of Hatshepsut. Available www.duke.edu/~drb3/hatshepsut/hatshepsut.html. Provides a good overview of Hatshepsut's reign, along with a diagram of her family tree.

Tomb Yields Mysteries of Ramses II, Salt Lake Tribune, October 7, 1997. Available www.sltrib.com/97/oct/100797/nation_w/781.htm. An Associated Press story that discusses the discovery of a tomb apparently built for the many sons of Ramses II.

INDEX

PICTURE CREDITS

ABOUT THE AUTHOR

Russell Roberts graduated from Rider University in Lawrenceville, New Jersey. A full-time freelance writer, he has published over 160 articles and short stories, and 5 previous nonfiction books: *Stolen: The Stolen Base in Baseball*, *Down the Jersey Shore*, *Discover the Hidden New Jersey*, *All About Blue Crabs and How to Catch Them*, and *Endangered Species*.

He currently resides in Bordentown, New Jersey, with his family and a lazy yet diabolical cat named Rusti.